T0194030

WHERE *is the* REAL CHURCH *of* GOD *in* CHRIST?

DR. CANDACE R. WILLIAMS

authorHOUSE

AuthorHouse™
1663 Liberty Drive
Bloomington, IN 47403
www.authorhouse.com
Phone: 1 (800) 839-8640

Published by AuthorHouse 07/07/2020

ISBN: 978-1-7283-6635-7 (sc)
ISBN: 978-1-7283-6633-3 (hc)
ISBN: 978-1-7283-6634-0 (e)

Library of Congress Control Number: 2020912459

Print information available on the last page.

Any people depicted in stock imagery provided by Getty Images are models, and such images are being used for illustrative purposes only. Certain stock imagery © *Getty Images.*

This book is printed on acid-free paper.

CONTENTS

NOTE TO THE READERS, HEARERS, AND DOERS

Be it known that all of the book contents are based on scriptures, personal experiences, and encounters. I am a born-again believer who believes in the death, burial, and resurrection of Jesus Christ, the authenticator of all things past, present and, future as well as the author and finisher of our faith.

With faith (full action in the house), we understand what pleases God. The God kind of faith is now. Without faith, it is impossible to please God because we must come believing that He is and that He is a rewarder of those who diligently seek Him.

This book is not just a good read but a testament of a life changed. The hearing and doing of the word of God brought liberation, making me free to echo what has already been retold from the foundation of the world.

This truth, as declared in the scriptures, will also liberate you. I trust that as you open these life-bringing pages, you will not want to put down this book. I believe you will come to be all the thirstier and hungrier for more as I have designed this life-changing book to bring an epiphany of the real church of God in Christ. Walk with me as we bring line upon line, precept upon precept, and revelation upon revelation as exposed by guidance of the Holy Spirit.

ACKNOWLEDGMENTS

Countless people have deposited into my spiritual bank, allowing me to have a constant and continual overflow to share from my experiences and encounters. I considered myself favored to have what I consider giants (great men and women) in the gospel to leave their imprint and influence my soul and spirit, giving me a thirst and hunger for the word of God. I could never have written this book without their impartation, guidance, and encouragement.

For many, time would not permit to name all who have helped me become who I am today and who I will be tomorrow. Their leadership then and even now continues to lend a hand to my overall development as being the church operating in the kingdom. I extend my dearest and profound appreciation to those in whom I am forever indebted to. I am unable to acknowledge everyone, but I wish to recognize a few people in particular.

First my children, Paris and Aaron, allowed me to be in the school of lifelong learning. They sacrificed their mother, allowing me to spend many days, nights, months, and years pursuing my passion to learn spiritual matters. My children didn't always understand my journey, the spiritual sacrifices, or struggles, but they knew God's hand was upon me and that I was *souled* out for God. I can't thank them enough for allowing me to be me.

I want to thank my spiritual father in the gospel, Bishop Malverse Simpson, and his wife, Elect Lady Rosalind Simpson, allowed the bishop to nurture me in the Spirit. I've been so fortunate to be given another spiritual father in the person of Dr. Anthony W. Hull Sr. whom I love dearly.

My family, friends, and ministry supporters have been there for me personally, professionally, and spiritually. They have allowed me to use my gifts and talents with and upon them. They have seeded into my ministry, believing and knowing that God called me out and up to do a work for Him. Thank you for your unswerving and effectual prayers over my life and the ministry that I am doing for God's glory.

Together we stand; divided we fall.

We're helpers one to another; I am my brother's keeper.

INTRODUCTION

This book speaks to the family of God. It will introduce to some and present to others an inside glimpse into the Bible's investigative truths. The goal is to expose the reality of where we are, where we're going, and how we will get there. It will also provide transparent moments: insight, hindsight, foresight, and oversight to the revelation and understanding of our identity, position, and purpose of the real church of God in Christ.

As you go deeper into this read, this ride may seem like a fast roller coaster, so I admonish you to buckle up because you will come to realize that it is a fast moving journey on the sponsorship of God's word.

Let us discover. Where is the real church of God in Christ?

CHAPTER 1

From Then to Now

Christianity has taken on various modalities in today's church. The church as we've known it has a change in appetite from the church of old. The church of old didn't have much materialistically. It wasn't in a better economic place or have the outward appearance of what this twenty-first-century church has. However, they had an authentic expression of love and fear of God, which seems to be somewhat different from what we see nowadays.

As we delve into this book, I will speak quite candidly on the things I've witnessed and heard along this way. I've noticed that today's church folk feel that the church of yesterday is just that … in the past! Modernization has caused so many to be less tolerant to information that they feel is obsolete, useless, and outdated. People are seeking a relevant, contemporary word and information that will change their situation and lives. The struggle is real for many who are trying to find out who they are, where they are, and what they are supposed to be doing, including when and how to get it done like right now. We, the real church of God in Christ, must show up being the solutionists and instruments that we're called to be so we can bring the masses back to the root of our existence until we produce the fruit of holiness and righteousness. This isn't just for us but for them.

Now in doing so on this journey, we've learned and have been eyewitnesses to the fact that some attempts by the preachers, students, theologians, scholars, and the like have come to some of the same conclusions. Their analytical developments regarding the origin of the church, its originator, and its functions—and of course where we are and where we are going—differ on many levels.

CHAPTER 2

Science, Fiction, or Truth

Various scientific and religious approaches introduce facts that say the church's origin is scientific in nature and that it was founded on human perception. In other words, if you can see it, then you can believe it. However, faith tells us if you believe it, you will surely see it.

Some have suggested that the church is nothing more than an organization or denomination with dutiful undertones. In other words, reformations are a process of reforming (to change or improve) an institution or practice. However, an insightful biblical perspective and true spiritual awareness and awakening will expose the true origin of the church as being founded on the authenticity of the word declared by John the revelator, who professed Jesus as the Alpha and Omega, the First and the Last, the Beginning and the End, the One who was, is, and is to come. This very Jesus provides the premise of what our lives should be within the boundaries of the Holy Scriptures and not the wisdom of humans.

We will come to learn that no matter how intellectually astute we are, how financially stable we may be, how socially connected we are, and how mentally and emotionally sound we think we are, the real church of God in Christ has a foundation that cannot be shaken, moved, or dethroned. You see, the church doesn't stand on its own accord. Its spiritual architectural firm has provided humanity a manual or blueprint that is active in the lives of people today, bringing about change to those who hear and do what is written therein.

We will come to grasp the truth that the church (contrary to scientific analogies) as founded in scripture is a living organism. The Greek word for organism, *organismos*, according to Wikipedia, is any individual entity that embodies the properties of life. It is a synonym for life-form.

This definition is what will speak and point to where the real church of God in Christ was, is, and will ever be: a living organism. In this, we find that any person, place, or thing that the real church of God in Christ comes in contact with will experience and encounter a *form change* from that which was the old to the new and improved through identity consciousness, according to 2 Corinthians 5:17–20 (emphasis mine).

> Therefore if any man be in Christ he is a new creature: old things are passed away; behold *all thing* are become new And all things are of God who hath reconciled us to himself by Jesus Christ and hath given to us the ministry of reconciliation God was in Christ reconciling the world unto himself not imputing their trespasses unto them and hath committed unto us the word of reconciliation Now then we are ambassadors for Christ.

What a powerful passage of scripture that reiterates the

initiation of all things! It started with God in Christ and will end with God in Christ. In this, we understand that the real church of God in Christ is built solely upon the redemptive work of Jesus Christ. "For there is no other way to come to the Father but by Him [Jesus]" (John 14:6). Colossians 1:18 echoes the truth that Jesus is declared to be "the head of the body, the church. He is the beginning, the firstborn from the dead, that in everything he might be preeminent." His preeminence is visibly seen over the course of His Story *(history)*.

Men and women of different nationalities, colors, creeds, ethnicities, religions, political systems, and the like have spent countless years trying to envision, comprehend, and predict heavenly things on earth. On my journey, I've encountered people who have shared in this same pursuit. Countless have shared testimonials of how they've come to gather biblical wisdom, knowledge, and understanding. Some have imparted what they've learned in and from their various ministries; others have expressed going through different training from seminaries of innumerable kinds, even attending schools of higher learning both near and abroad. Now some have felt that time was of the essence and they needed to take a three-day journey in one day. In doing this, some have reported maximizing that time by utilizing this modern-day technological age to bring them biblical data at the tip of their fingers. What a power move! However, if this power of technology isn't grounded, it too can become a portal of corruption and demonically inspired entries for many, as we can clearly see now.

Theological knowledge gained from these countless mediums

of educational studies and utilization of techno devices has caused some that I know to now consider themselves experts from their repertoire and spiritual revelatory knowledge base. Titles, positions, influence, clichés, zip codes, cars, houses, and sizes of houses have become the goals, destinations, and new norms in some circles of Christendom. There is this newly learned behavior that is manifesting in the church arenas. People feel the need to clone the greatest dancers, mimic others' tongues, obtain the messages and knowledge of others, and simply go through the motions of what they have seen modeled and imitated before them. Much of this has simply been counterfeits of the real.

Unfortunately those same dances and tongues that have been practiced haven't been able to keep the person(s) living a righteous and holy life as a believer should demonstrate. We can certainly learn the dos and don'ts from one another, but we must apply the spiritual knowledge we've gained so we may grow in the grace given us. However, I am a bit taken aback that we as a people can become so far removed from the grace for that place.

We have been given an opportunity to gain vital heart-changing information, but unfortunately some use it for the wrong reasons. You see, knowledge puffs us, but charity will lift us.

Pause as I share a transparent moment. When I was in college, I had to take a humanities course. As I scoped out my options, I saw a class in biblical studies. I was excited in thinking this would be a push for my own personal desire to learn more about spiritual matters. I initially assumed the people in the class had the same desires as I did.

Next, I assumed that this would be a chance for me to see an example of a community of believers in a secular educational system and the professor would have a passion for teaching the scriptures and, most of all, would live by them. Unfortunately I quickly learned as the class evolved that not everyone was there for the same reasons.

I admit I was zealous and a bit green on spiritual matters at the time in my life, simply assuming things that weren't even close to the reality I was about to experience. I learned that some were there for the following reasons: they needed the three credits so they could graduate, the other courses were already filled and this was the last option, or they wanted to debate their beliefs with others.

Now during this educational escapade, the participants' expectation called for the use of a specific Bible with utilization and inclusion of non-canonized books. In other words, these books were written but had no authenticity and were not considered divinely inspired. However, I was able to push through religiosity and continue my pursuit of truth. I found myself wanting more and was being challenged for more, much like what is about to be shared in this book. There is yet a pursuit to attain an understanding of the evolution of spiritual/ biblical substance. This search has become a high commodity in this modern day.

As aforementioned, many have a thirst for spiritual understanding and knowledge, but not all will want it for the purpose it was given. Nonetheless, may this book whet your appetite as you choose to stay in hot pursuit to the foundational principles for the reason we have our very existence as the real church of God in Christ. Now let me just say for those who are under the reformation of church of God in Christ, this book isn't about church of God in Christ, but as you read on, you will see that what it is about and rejoice.

In this new age where information can be obtained almost faster than a person can speak it via all these smart devices such as your phone and TV, it causes people to be more inquisitive than in times past. People are emerging with many questions from the hard drive of their minds. They are in search of answer and solutions, a means to an end.

CHAPTER 3

Laying the Foundation

To get a means to an end, you will come to know that the church has been in existence for over two thousand years. God spoke in Genesis 1 by the word of His power. When He spoke the word, the Spirit moved.

John 1:1 tells us, "In the beginning was the Word, and the Word was with God, and the Word was God." This same word brought redemption for the existence and birth of the real church of God in Christ. Hebrews 11:9 - 10 reveals that "by faith he (Abraham), sojourned in the land of promise as in a strange country dwelling in tabernacles with Isaac and Jacob the heirs with him of the same promise". Abraham diligently searched out and looked for a city with permanent foundations whose architect and builder is God.

Abraham was a tent dweller, as many were in that day, but by his faith in God (not faith in faith), he would come to find that this foundational promise wasn't temporal but everlasting because it wasn't made by the hands of mankind.

2 Corinthians 5:1 testifies as to what Abraham's faith move declares to us. "For we know; (in other words, we are intimate with the truth) that if our earthly house of this tabernacle were dissolved (torn down, demolished, disrupted), we have a building fashioned by the hand of God eternal in the heavens."

Hebrews 3:4 sums it up, reminding us that "every house is built by some man, but he that builds all things is God." Now that's a "tested, precious, and sure foundation" (Isaiah 28:16). I've got happy right there. Glory!

CHAPTER 4

The Meaning of the Word "Church"

So what then is the church? The meaning of the word "church" is derived from the Old Testament Hebrew word *Qahal*, which means an assembly of the chosen people of God. The Greek word in the New Testament for our English word "church" is *ekklesia*.

This multifarious Greek preface word *ek* means "out." *Kaleo* means "to call or summon." The literal meaning is "to call out." There are debates in the intellectual and religious sect about the word *Ekklesia* being a representative of the church. However, for this purpose, that isn't here or there as it relates to what our focus is intended to bring about. Now looking at the church's preciseness, we've concluded that an examination is a summon to order of those "called out." The question is, "Called out to what? Called out for what?"

In the research or discovery for the answers to such a valiant question, we find many people, places, and things that have tried to replace, reduce, and even attempt to restructure the church. What do we mean by this? The authoritative biblical principles from times past and even now have been based on truth, not facts, as it relates to the scriptures. The scriptures haven't changed because our tolerance has changed for truth.

We're in a day where some would try to flip the scriptures to suit their own agendas, purposes, and plans. However, although there have been many attempts of humanity to readjust the light, change the lighting, or bring the lighting upon oneself, it still won't dim the true light that cometh into the world. No one then or now can! The church of the living God was not built upon mere humankind concoctions, monumental ideas, philosophical gesticulations, or terrestrial positions, but upon another prophetic revelation given to Peter in Matthew 16:16, "Thou are the Christ, the Son of the Living God."

Upon the release and hearing of Peter's confession, Jesus responded by first telling Peter Simon Barjona that he was blessed (happy/fortunate). What a blessing to know that you're declared blessed. Luke 1:28 says "And the angel came in unto her, and said, Hail, Thou that are highly favored, the Lord is with thee: blessed art thou among women." That's enough to praise Him right there.

Matthew 16: 16 - 17 reports "And Simon Peter answered and said, Thou art the Christ, the Son of the living God. And Jesus answered and said unto him, Blessed art thou, Simon Barjona" for flesh and blood hath not revealed it unto thee, but my Father which is in heaven." Jesus then gave Peter his identity as Petros GK, which means a fragment of a rock/stone. Jesus wanted Peter to know that he was a fragment of the rock/stone, but not the rock or stone. Jesus himself was the rock in a weary land, a stone whom the builder's rejected became the capstone, headstone, or cornerstone (Psalm 118:22).

Jesus reveals this revelatory glimpse into this spiritual impression by stating to Peter in Matthew 16:18 that on his confession, "Thou are the Christ." "I will build my church; and the gates of hell shall not prevail against it." Before we get into this awesome prophetic revelation given to Peter, it is important to understand according to 2 Timothy 3:16–17, "All scripture is God breath and is profitable for doctrine, for reproof, for correction, for instruction in righteousness: that the man of God may be perfect, thoroughly furnished unto all good works."

Therefore, we must be open to understand scriptural interpretation as written knowledge according to 2 Peter 1:20–1, "no prophecy of scripture is of any private interpretation ... but spoken by holy men of God as the Spirit inspired them to speak." For this reason, this summation will provide a comprehensive representation of the focus of the real church of God in Christ from scripture to scripture.

We must also understand when the Bible speaks of the church, it is not referring to a literal building, erection, or infrastructure or a denomination, organization, or incorporation under human authority. The people of God are the embodied church. In other words, if Christ in us is the hope of glory, we then personify the inward/outward expression of the real church of God in Christ boldly.

So just where did the church derive from? Where did it all begin? To answer such questions, it would be wise for us to look subjectively and objectively to its origin. However, to appreciate the church's origin, one must have a clear and concise understanding of the foundation from which the origin of the church stands.

Apostle Paul wrote a letter to the church of Corinth to help them comprehend the essence of the church's stability.

We've discussed a bit of this earlier, but it warrants a deeper look as founded in 1 Corinthians 3:10–11. Apostle Paul states, "According to the grace of God which is given unto me as a wise master builder, I have laid the foundation, and another buildeth thereon. But let every man take heed how he buildeth thereupon." He then summarizes this thought in verse 11 by ensuring the church's foundation is as solid as a rock. "For no other foundation can no man lay than that is laid, which is Jesus Christ."

Psalm 11:3 says, "If the foundation be destroyed, what can the righteous do?" For this reason, we must realize that although the apostles and prophets laid the church's foundation, the source of all that is laid is God through faith in Jesus Christ. 2 Timothy 2:19 sums it up, "Nevertheless, the foundation of God standeth sure." In other words, the real church of God in Christ cannot be moved. Many have tried, but they never have and never will succeed.

A great man of God I know made a very profound statement, "The Old Testament is the New Testament concealed, the New Testament is the Old Testament revealed." In other words, the Old Testament is like our shadow, but when the Son is revealed, so then is the image.

What a powerful, discerning word! Therefore, to understand the next segments of thoughts, it is necessary to note the connection between that which was to that which is.

The Old Testament predictions declare the approaching of the foundational stone, which points to Jesus. The church as originated in the scripture was birthed out of Jesus's spiritual matrix, which has been proven that though it may experience difficulties, challenges, and setbacks, it cannot and will not ever be overthrown, ruined, dissimulated, or dismantled. Jesus the Christ is absolute. The word *absolute* simply means existing independently, not relatively or comparatively. Nothing happens in, on, above, under, or around this earth that He isn't aware of.

Ephesians 2:20 – 22 reveals the identity and connection of the people thusly declaring NOW… not later, not soon to come, not in the sweet by and by; but "NOW therefore ye are no more strangers and foreigners, but follow-citizens with the saints and of the household of God; And are built upon the foundation of the apostles and prophets, Jesus Christ himself being the chief corner stone; in whom all the building fitly framed together growth unto an holy temple in the Lord: In whom ye also are builded together for an habitation of God through the Spirit."

In other words, as a member of the body we recognize we belong to God and should always be presented a God's dwelling place, where he resides. What a powerful text simply declares! When our lives are one in Christ, we become builders upon that same foundation.

Colossians 3:3 reminds the believers "for ye are dead; and your life is hid with Christ in God." Therefore, we must understand and exemplify Ephesians 3:9 by "helping everyone, not some, but ALL to see how this secret that has been at work was hidden for all ages by God, who created all things." However, the secret is out! It is revealed by the birthing of the church through the shed blood of Jesus's death, burial, and resurrection.

Roman 1:3–4 provides the framework and biblical truths that Jesus was a descendant of David with respect to his humanity. He was declared by the resurrection from the dead to be the powerful Son of God according to the spirit of holiness.

Jesus is the Messiah, our Lord. When we know that according to John 14:6 that this same Jesus is declared the "I AM the way, the truth and the life," regardless of how people attempt to bring obscurity to the vision of some by presenting facts, truth continues to prevail. Let's see this truth in action.

CHAPTER 5

The Origin and Head of the Church

In the study of the origin and head of the church, we will have an all-embracing conversation of the two parts. We must take a glimpse back to understand the now of the real church of God in Christ. First, let's look at the church. The church, if I could paint a picture, is like a body, as apostle Paul explained. It has many parts that work conjointly together for the overall good of its global purpose. 1 Corinthians 12:14 says, "For the body is not one member, but many." Every part has its own functionality that grows into a lively stone when properly connected. The church is visible, universal, and movable, but let me pause right there to share where some think it all started.

Some believe the church emerged at Pentecost. Now I've since learned not to assume anything but bring a base investigation and explanation from what the scriptures speaks to. In a study of the scriptures, I've learned that Pentecost was one of the Jewish festivals called "Shavuot," which depicted the spring harvest festival for the Israelites. And it is said that Shavuot marks a time when the Tarah was given to Moses on Mount Sinai. It is considered a pivotal event in Israelites' history. Pentecost comes about fifty days after Passover.

The Passover was another breakthrough in the Israelites' history. During this time, many observances were held such as special prayer, refraining from labor, and preparation of special meals. Passover is also known as *Pesach*, a Hebraic language that was sacred for the Jews. It was a holiday that lasted about seven days as the feast of unleavened bread. This was symbolic and a shadow of what was coming in the person of Jesus. Jesus was that Passover lamb. He even declared, "I AM the Bread of God and of Life" (John 6:33–35).

In other words, Jesus was being revealed as the Israelites were on the move and had no time to wait for their bread to rise, but they had to be ready and prepared to make their transition when called upon by their leader, staying mentally and physically mobile. The leader Moses was instructed to kill the sacrificial lamb and have the people place the blood upon the doorpost, so the death angel may pass by. In this interchange, the Israelites would come to witness judgment upon their enemies in Egypt.

This fearless act represented the finale of the ten plagues where the firstborn would die. That ultimate plague descended upon Egyptian land, providing an announcement to the benediction of Pharaoh agreeing to let the Israelites go so they may go and become the people God was calling them to become. So as mentioned, as the people of God transitioned, Pentecost would become the next essential manifestation of the change, shifting and lifting of the church coming into power.

In Luke 24:49, Jesus said "And, behold, I send the promise of my Father upon you: but tarry ye in the city of Jerusalem; until ye be endued with power from on high."

In other words, this simply meant to sit, or what I call "wait" (why I am talking). They needed to be still (immobile) where the only sound heard would be their prayers. They had to wait in Jerusalem, which represents the city of God until they be endued (cloth upon or put upon) power from on high.

Now this power didn't originate from humans; nor could it ever be. It was the supernatural power that once was revealed as a bush that burned but not consumed, a pillar of cloud by day and fire by night that moved from being an external manifestation to a pure, internal representation of power released in and upon the people of God at Pentecost. The followers gathered together understood the word that John baptized with water, but they would be baptized with the Holy Ghost not many days hence.

Acts 1:8 tells us "But ye shall receive power, after that the Holy Ghost is come upon you: and ye shall be witnesses unto me both in Jerusalem, and in all Judaea, and in Samaria and unto the uttermost part of the earth." So we learn that those who were in the waiting room would receive power after the Holy Ghost came upon them and they would be witnesses. The waiting room thus becomes a place of expectancy, a site where there would be an internal igniting. Approximately 120 persons in the upper room would experience this encounter of being filled with the indwelling of the Holy Spirit. However, it would not stop there. This supernatural fire was introduced at Pentecost, but many thereafter, even until now by faith in the death, burial, resurrection, and ascension of Jesus, would also be partakers.

Jesus didn't just get up. He rose up and stayed up. The book of Acts—or what some calls the Acts of the Apostle and other Acts of the Holy Spirit—would become the birthing of the rising of the real church of God in Christ in power, but not in existence. Pentecost would be the exhibition of the promised.

According to the scripture flow, we find that though the church was manifested in power, it was first declared by a revelatory word spoken by the one who would be sacrificed as a lamb slain before the foundation of the world. Therefore, the church origin at Pentecost becomes debatable for some.

Some have expressed that the origin of the church falls somewhere between the garden of Eden to the day of Pentecost. However, just as it was in the beginning according to Genesis 1, "God spoke the Spirit moved." So, it is now. However, what He spoke became the autopsy to the basis of the origin. God spoke the word. According to John 1:1, Jesus was that word manifestly declared from the beginning. When the Holy Spirit heard the word, He was moved to action. This is certainly true, even with the origin of the church.

Genesis 3:15 provides a prophetic backdrop of the coming attraction, letting us know that when man fell through disobedience, a sentence was declared, therefore initiating the seed of the church that would be produced in the woman. Genesis 3:15 says "And I will put enmity between thee and the woman, and between thy seed and her seed; it shall bruise thy head, and thou shalt bruise his heel." So historically speaking, the prophetic seed would become the headliners of major and minor prophetic voices throughout generations. The prophet Isaiah would declare a question in Isaiah 53:1, "Who has believer our message, and to who has the arm of the Lord been revealed?" He would continue this discourse, setting forth who would move centuries ahead as a tender plant until we see the appearance of the real church of God in Christ emerging from that seed that bursts forth as a shoot out of dry ground.

Now catch the revelation, and you will then see the full image. So, to talk about the origin of the church, you must talk about the seed carrier. Mary, the mother of Jesus, was overshadowed by the Holy Spirit (Matthew 1:18) to bring forth the promised child. It amazes me when I think of the impregnation and birth of Christ. Mary would come to see that the very one she was carrying would soon be carrying her and us.

Jesus would arise on the scene not in form or fashion, but a lowly one who would be despised and rejected, a man of sorrows intimately familiar with suffering. He would not be what people were looking for, but certainly what they needed. The people would hide their faces. They despise and devalue Him, as prophet Isaiah declared in Isaiah 53.

Jesus was presented as an average Joe. He didn't come with an entourage. He didn't have a social media following or make flyers. He didn't have cash app or PayPal. He didn't do the network thing. He showed up and out, presenting who He was, truth in action.

He healed the sick, raised the dead, and caused the lame to walk and the dumb to talk. He unstopped deaf ears and opened blinded eyes. When He spoke, He captivated the people greater than any other ever could. He brought hope to the hopeless, had compassion on the multitudes, and spoke life to many. He did not perform miracles, signs, and wonders only, but He was the epitome of them. Jesus showed Himself alive after His passion by many infallible proofs, being seen of them forty days, speaking things pertaining to the kingdom of God.

So the origin of the real church of God in Christ has a rich history and origin that still is developing in the lives of people all over the world. One thing is known as we see a piece of this historic origin manifesting through the word Jesus declared unto Peter. This prophetic reveal is spoken in Matthew 16:17 upon Peter's revelation, "Thou are the Christ, the Son of the Living God," which sealed Jesus's response. He said, "Flesh and blood has not revealed this to you ... but my Father which is in heaven."

This declaration was a game-changer. It was not just a personal revelation spoken by God to Peter. It was an inauguration or launching thereof that unearths the real church of God in Christ through the personhood of Jesus. It is undoubtedly scriptural evidence that compels one to believe and understand the significance of what God had given.

Even from times of old, the prophecies spoke of He who would come and die for the sins of the world, foreshadowing what was about to be the reality. Isaiah 6:9 states, "For unto us a child is born a son is given." It is important to note this text as we move forward into the appreciation to what was given. A child was born, but a Son was given. This is phenomenal! A child is not able to make a choice to be sacrificed; however, a son who has matured to obedience can surrender to his God-given purpose.

Hebrew 5:8 tells us, "Though he was a son, he learned obedience through the things he suffered." So we understand that the power of God is unto salvation through faith in Jesus Christ, "the only begotten of the Father full of grace and truth" (John 1:14). It is elating each time I think about the sacrifice given that birth forged the real church of God in Christ. That's why it's necessary and only befitting to state what the church is not.

CHAPTER 6

What the Church Is "Not"

Contrary to popular demand and the religious status quo, my journey has led me to understand that some churches have yet to be established on a solid biblical foundation. Some simply have been built upon human traditions and opinions, but not upon Christ Himself and the eternal word. How do we know this? The apostle Paul declared in 1 Corinthians 2:1–5 what I believe sets a precedence to the demonstration of the whole matter. "When he came to the brothers with God's secret it wasn't with rhetorical language or wisdom."

Paul brought clarity of his message, reiterating it wasn't with clever or wise words but by the display of the power of the Spirit of God. Paul said this to let them know that their faith shouldn't be based on human wisdom, but the power of God.

So many today rely on their education above their meditation. However, when we show up as the real church of God in Christ exposed as the light of the world, we realize it is not us, but the power of God working through us. We take no credit for anything as we realize we are nothing without God and can do nothing apart from Him. It is in Mark 7:13 the actions wherewith Jesus spoke saying "Making the word of God of none effect through your tradition…" Colossians 2:8 says, "Beware lest any man spoil you through philosophy and vain deceit after the tradition of men, after the rudiments of the world and not after Christ. In other words, some uphold the law, rites, rituals, ideology, earthly knowledge/wisdom, and traditions even above the truth. Jesus again declared one of His infamous I AMs, "I AM the WAY, TRUTH and LIFE" (John 14).

Isaiah 45:23 tells us, "By myself I have sown—from my mouth has gone out integrity, a promise that won't be revoked: To me every knee will bow, and every tongue will sware." Then Hebrews 6:13 reverberates, "When God made his promise to Abraham, since there was no one greater for him to swear by, he swore by himself." Mighty is our God.

So the apostle Paul found himself dealing with the counterattack of the traditionists and religious people of his time. He remained focused as he brought encouragement and education to the people, as seen in Colossians 2:8, "Beware any man spoil you through philosophy and vain deceit, after the tradition of men, after the rudiments of the world, and not after Christ," due to the tradition of men, wives' fables, people having itchy ears, and those making false declarations of what they perceive the church to be. It is visibly seen that the church of the living God as found in scripture is vastly different in its characteristics that religiosity and traditional viewpoints say. Unfortunately, some have cloaked their traditional understandings by giving unjustified demands to the people in their congregations that have no biblical values and substance.

Some of these needless gestures have brought the people of God back into bondage even worse than that of Pharaoh, Herod, and the like. Apostle Paul spoke up in Galatians 5, demanding a response to his question to the Galatians. "Who have bewitched you?"

In other words, who have you allowed to cast a spell on you? Who have you allowed to speak in and enter in your ear and heart gate, turning you away from the truth? We see these same kinds of things still happening in the real church of God in Christ today. However, we've become bougie in some of our churches, forgetting from whence we've come.

What do I mean? Bougie people are those who are pretentious and snooty. They put on airs and think they are better than others, elevated in a higher class. Even some leaders in the various reformations will give you a high seat if you look, talk, and act the part.

Some of them have become spiritual fashion police, looking at you from head to toe when you enter their sanctuary. They act as if they are discerning but are really checking you out for other reasons and motives. If you are dressed in the latest fashionable attire, then you can fit into their elite group. If you are a big giver, then you can have preferred seating or a high seat. Can I tell you that high seats are for toddlers? We've shifted from having high seats to having thrones. Two kings can't occupy the same throne or kingdom. Ponder on this.

Some have said that you must be in God's authoritative hierarchy of what is called the fivefold ministry of an apostle, prophet, evangelist, pastor, or teacher to be perceived as somebody special in their upper-echelon assemblies. Oh, but the latest in these many forms of bondage is having a title or set position. Unfortunately, some people feel entitled and sense that they are superior to others; therefore they will secretly pay to obtain these titles. They join what some could say are secret societies right in the house of God.

These secret societies are for the elite with benefits. You are invited to specific functions and private meetings. You can sit in certain places (often high seats or on thrones) among the who's who in the church. Some of these people will do anything to get in where they can fit in. They will not only pay (seeding big offerings), but they will also lay (sleep with whoever, whatever, wherever, whenever, and however) to obtain these titles and positions. Some will also betray (have secret meetings about you after getting information on you) and then stray to other reformations to obtain these titles, positions, and prestige. I would even daresay some who are desperate to get notoriety will even slay (kill your influence).

In this day and time, titles up for grabs are that of an archbishop, master prophet, or doctor. We understand that many things can and will be bestowed upon, vocalized and considered to be traits of the church; therefore, walk with me on my soapbox that will continue to reveal and define what the church is not.

The real church of God in Christ is not a cult. Merriam-Webster says that a cult is "a system of religious beliefs and rituals." The church is not just a place where people gather as a social club, hook up with clique networks, or try to get a physical hookup with the next boo or bae. It is not just a place to dance and shout. The Bible says in 1 Timothy 4:8, "bodily exercises profits little: but godliness is profitable unto all thing having the promise of the life that now is, and of that which is to come."

Now don't get me wrong. You should not only feel God's presence when you're in the assembly of the righteous; you should respond to His presence at least sometimes. However, many are shouting, speaking in tongues, touching their neighbors, and saying you're coming out when they've been trapped for some time. They look like they are free, delivered, and healed, but they are often betrayed by their lifestyles and their own speech.

Now here's what I believe: I believe that those same tongues that cause you to quicken and shake and those same dances that cause you to pick them up and put them down ought to be the same that cause you to live a holy and righteous lifestyle. We have a lot of people in Christendom who are exemplifying various practices of things that they've been told is the appearance of the real church, but truthfully, we will come to learn that the real church of God in Christ is more than tongues, a dance, and having a high time in the Lord (whatever that means). Here's the thing: we may dance and shout, but we are oftentimes simply left with a sweating out of our clothes and hair, but no real change or deliverance.

The real church of God in Christ will bring transformation to your life and change to your mind. What you used to do, you won't have an appetite to do it again. Your wrongdoing and thinking will repulse you. You'll hate what God hates and love what He loves.

You'll come to know that to stay righteous and holy, you must be connected and stay connected to the righteous and

Holy One! The real church of God in Christ is not a place for the exercise of great minds or the intellectual astuteness of men and women. "Knowledge puffeth up, but charity edifies" (1 Corinthians 8:1). In other words, some people have obtained knowledge both secularly and spiritually, and trust me, I am all for upgrading your educational attainments, but your meditation will be more suitable in spiritual matters. Furthermore, if you are not grounded in truth according to authorship of biblical principles, these same men and women can get a big head. What do I mean? You won't be able to tell them anything. They know it all. They've seen it all and done it all.

Listen, we haven't come out to the world to act like the world is competing against one other. We're not here to see who can outhoop, outpreach, outpray, outprophesy, outsing, or outplay the instruments and the like. The real church of God in Christ is not a place to become content and comfortable seated in soft, padded pews or chairs, losing focus at the beauty of the edifices and the glistening of the chandeliers. You aren't to be mesmerized at the stained-glass windows. You don't leave your footprint on the plush, fashionable carpet patterns. You aren't getting sidetracked by lights-camera-action formation.

I've experienced going into a church that displayed a good name but had mad game. I didn't know if I were at a disco or club because the lighting went up at certain intervals of the services and down for the other. I thought, *Cut out all the lights so we can see what is really going on up in here, from the pulpit to the door.*

We are inundated with the latest technological devices that

we may experience a certain sound and look that may become the projection of the ministry that we now call the spirit of excellence. Now I have no desire to go, look, think, or act back or do anything backward because I believe the real church of God in Christ is a progressive church.

However, a glance back is necessary from time to time so you won't forget. I remember when we read the announcements off a piece of paper we just picked up or a bulletin we made up. Now we just flash them on our seventy-inch televisions using our techno remotes and devices. I recall the musicians played so under the anointing and unction of the Holy Ghost that the very sound and wind of the Spirit had you slain in the Spirit. Nobody had to lay hands on you or even say anything to you. The leaders would allow the Holy Ghost to do the work.

It's a transparent moment. I remember the day I was filled with the Holy Ghost. It was an experience I had never had but had heard about. I went to a revival at this small church that honestly looked like the size of my living room. This little elderly preacher brought a message of salvation that night.

While I listened to what he said, I had various complaints about my life as he made the altar call. He spoke these words as I made my way out of the pews saying, "Come seeking what you will from the Lord." As I said, I had so many complaints about how my life had seemed to be more challenging than it was before I was saved. In my mind, I began reminiscing and comparing what I had to what I have in that moment.

I was struggling, emotionally, mentally, and spiritually. I wanted to see the manifestation of God but also desired to know how my situation would change. Suddenly I heard a still, small voice pose a question, calling me by my name. Although I was in a crowded room, I didn't see or hear anyone else in that moment. Then after what appeared in times past, I heard one of the mothers of the church say, "I see the fire." Then she pointed at me and said, "Receive ye the Holy Ghost."

I opened my mouth to continue where I left off in my complaint, but out of my mouth I began to speak in tongues as the Spirit gave utterance. There were no musicians, yet I heard melodies from heaven playing beautiful sounds from the Spirit as I laid on the floor weeping before the presence of God, speaking in my heavenly language.

Now I've witnessed people getting thrills from musicians playing unholy chords in a holy sanctuary as if we don't know. The funny thing is that people are often clapping, swaying, singing, and dancing to the beat of a different sound that doesn't represent the real church of God in Christ.

Musicians are not only gifted but should be tune in with the Spirit. Playing chords that causes an atmosphere to be conducive for the power of God to be made manifested. Created atmospheres that drives out demons, release healing and deliverance. Musicians then and now are a bit different. Musicians then were servants as with the preacher. Now people have become hirelings being sold out rather than being *souled out*.

We've come to understand that some who say they are of the fold can become quite satisfied with the outward signs of what they know and see the church being and becoming, that is, the appearance thereof. I remember going into a church, and as soon as I stepped foot in, I heard the Holy Ghost say to me, "Appearance."

What I was looking at didn't have the outward expressions of the real church of God in Christ, but simply an appearance, a form, if you will. 2 Timothy 3:5 says that people will "have a form (an outward formation, façade, or a front with an appearance) of godliness, but deny the power thereof." People will appear to look the part of true holiness, but their lifestyles will speak something totally different. These people will be on the usher, deacon, and mother boards. They will be on the front rows, in the pulpit or choir stands, and on the instruments. However, Paul tells us to stay away from such people.

Unfortunately we see these things (fog, flashing, and smoky lights) yet happening in the modernized church gatherings. They will have the latest fashionable structures, names in big lights, and connective associations and congregations, but I can tell you that most of those things are a cover-up and superficial presentations. They still do not represent or define the real church of God in Christ. There are artificial sounds that claim to be of the Spirit but are not. They are sounding brass and making tinkling cymbals, a bunch of noise that does not magnify or exemplify our Lord or His purpose for the church.

These too are only representations of artificial displays of what may be pleasing and acceptable to man but are certainly not always the glowing attributes of our Lord Church. God is pleased when a life is lived by faith and obedience to Him above gifts, talents, and treasure.

Listen, we've talked briefly about this already, but you must know that the church is not an organization, denomination, or business. However, some of the workings or functionalities of these three are generally used in daily administration and operations of the church, but understand they are not the church. An organization brings together people with a specific purpose for the connection. It provides basic structure and production of what the work requires and how the work is to be done.

A denomination is basically a self-governing entity within a religious sect. In other words, a denomination is a subgroup of a larger group or culture with commonalities and/or trademarks that speak to their identity and connections.

This is much like the churches of God in Christ: the Church of God, Full Gospel, Bibleway, Apostolic, Word of Faith, Baptist, AME, Methodist, Presbyterian, Pentecostal circles, Assemblies of the World, and the likes. New reformations are rising up, just too many to keep up with. Many of these reformations have subcultures within the constructs of what they believe. Not all their operations express themselves the same, although they have some shared commonalities and functionalities.

Now I've personally been a part of a few of these reformations on my journey and have seen firsthand that though they may be under the same umbrella, they function independently until for the most part there is a coming together, like at their conferences. At these conferences, you begin to see a united front being demonstrated on the scenes, but behind the scenes, there is yet a visible difference displayed.

Nonetheless, we come to understand that the church is

neither that which is solely natural but spiritual in nature. The church is an organism, a living being. An organism is described or defined as any living thing that develops by inherent life, according to Merriam-Webster. This basically means the sum total of related parts, in which the relationship of each part to part involves a relationship to the whole. This wholeness can only be obtained through our faith in Jesus Christ where nothing is missing, broken, or lacking.

Now that we have an understanding, we see that the real church of God in Christ is a movable, transitional church that involves and evolves to reveal Jesus, our centerpiece. You see, the real church of God in Christ was never designed to be a monument, but a movement. I lived in a city where there was a location called Monument Boulevard. On this boulevard stood figurines and statues of historical people up and down this location.

One day as I rode down this boulevard, I began to get a revelation through the Spirit about the difference between a monument and a movement. I came to learn that a monument remained a symbol of what was, used to be, but lacks mobility. A monument represented that of the past. However, a movement represented that which is in transit and present. As I looked around and observed, various modes of transportation going were before and after those stationary monuments. So it is with the real church of God in Christ. We are not stationary as a monument, but we are a people on the move.

We are no longer tent dwellers using that which is temporal, but as New Testament believers, we continue to move from glory to glory, faith to faith, and strength to strength, all by the Spirit of God. We are not only a church on the move, we come to know that we have a specific direction in which we are moving toward—forward and up. We are moving by advancing in the work and purpose of the church functioning and advancing in the kingdom.

CHAPTER 7

The Work and Purpose of the Church

The crux of our Christian duty can be summed up in one word, missions, for this is God's appointed means of our work and purpose for the advancement of the kingdom. It is the duty set forth in the Great Commission. Too often churches lose sight of this purpose. Their "light" is turned wholly inward, and all things are often directed at the individual and corporate level, presenting as pleasures and comforts. We too often become comfortable in our ministries, churches, and places of worship to the degree that we're not working the works. We cease to be witnesses of spiritual matters because we get caught up in the cares of this world, which leads to self-indulgence and spiritual laziness when it comes to doing the work of the ministry and not just the work in the ministry.

The work in the ministry is that of parking attendant, greeter, usher, praise and worship leader, security, financier, intercessor, and so on. These and many more are functionalities of the working inside the ministry. However, the work of the ministry extends beyond the four walls of any building. The work of the ministry is where in-reach shifts to outreach.

In this transition, it requires in the making of a disciple (who becomes and are student/learners) who are spiritually developed by the reading, studying, and teaching of the word. This is also where preparation meets opportunity. In other words, the congregants or members of that local body is equipped with the tools to go beyond the doors of the church, shifting their focus training from activation to demonstration through the vehicle of outreach.

So what is outreach? Outreach is when a group within the faith community or church (not a person/individual only) puts foot to their faith, going into the communities and sharing the good news while meeting the needs of that community. Now there are many ways to demonstrate outreach, for instance, feeding, clothing, providing shelter, and offering community events that inspire, lift, and encourage the people. In other words, outreach brings hope while bridging the gap. In addition, outreach provides community resources of various kinds, which again speaks to the necessities of that community while arising in its agenda, demonstrating the real love of God that has drawing power.

This is every believer's instructions to the fulfillment of what Jesus spoke unto his disciples as they traveled to Galilee in Matthew 28:16–20. Jesus told them four things to do in verse 19 that speaks to the works of the Great Commission, which is for kingdom purpose:

"Go ye therefore, and teach all nations, baptizing them in the name of the Father and of the Son and of the Holy Ghost: Teaching them to observe all things whatsoever I have commanded you: and, lo, I am with you always, even unto the end of the world. Amen." The reassurance is that they are not alone in the work.

Now it is interesting that the first command given to the disciples for their purpose was "go." The real church of God in Christ isn't just sitting in their beautiful facilities waiting, hoping, and praying that the people will just show up at their doors.

They understand the assignment and commission is for them to go, to get up and do something. You see, Jesus was reiterating the concept that the real church of God in Christ, the church that He built, has always been mobile and in motion. The word "go" simply means to move. It is a verb, an action word that leads to animation. We are commissioned to go, which leads me to my next train of thought.

Know this: we are not going haphazardly, without direction, purpose, or power. As aforementioned, the real church of God in Christ was fully equipped for their purpose, much like what apostle Paul shared with Timothy in 2 Timothy 4:5(b). The apostle tells his protégé Timothy, "But watch thou in all things endure afflictions, do the work of an evangelist, make full proof of thy ministry." You see, Timothy was a young pastor about to step into his assignment of Pastoring a large ministry in which he needed the guidance of a mentor. So, Paul provided guided instructions to him to be alert, calm, and collected in spirit. You see, when you are sharing God's love with anyone, you must be discerning and compassionate. So, apostle Paul says secondly, "endure afflictions." In doing the work of the ministry, participating in the Great Commission, you must know that you may not always be received by those whom you are sharing God's love with.

Let me pause right there. Some people have been hurt and abused by others who profess Christ in and out of the church building. These occurrences happen in gatherings of all sorts (from workplaces, communities, and even in the home and churches).

Although you may have not been the one who brought the infliction to that person, as a member of the body of Christ because of your connections, you thus become indirectly a part of the presenting issues, complaints, and pain they have.

However, as a result, these persons become guarded. In other words, they are sometimes a bit quick-tempered, touchy, and sensitive to what or who is speaking. They discharge their multitude of complaints and oftentimes want answers from the presenter of "Why?"

Can we be honest here? We do realize that some of their complaints are valid. They did experience what they did, and we do not want to ignore this fact or take away what they feel. People feel what they feel, they know what they know, and they will say what they want to say about it. However, we, on the other hand, want to actively listen and hear them out as this becomes a problem when we don't, which validates their complaints all the more. We don't want to find ourselves making excuses or trying to explain away what that person who brought those mental, emotional, and spiritual infractions did or said to that person.

Nevertheless, we need the spirit of wisdom and revelation to rest upon us so in our responses as the real church of God in Christ, we will know when to hold them, fold them, and pray for them without thus exacerbating their open wounds. Sometimes you simply may have to just move on, of course continuing to pray that God will move upon, soften, and heal their hearts.

Now we find in clause (b) the apostle tells the young Timothy to "do the work of an evangelist, make full proof (discharge and devote yourself completely) to thy ministry." So what is the work of the evangelist?

Well, first know that this person (the evangelist) can be male or female who brings good tidings or good news to people with urgency. The real church of God in Christ must also act with this same urgency concerning the work and purpose for which we as believers are called. So know we have the baseline of the work, but the question remains: Why does it seem the church is failing in this purpose?

CHAPTER 8

Whose Responsibility Is It?

Can I propose the responsibility and issue starts at the individual level? In other words, that lack of personal responsibility and accountability as a member of the body of Christ is coupled with a dependence upon others to make or take up this slack, becoming a case of chronic shirking of duty. Individual irresponsibility produces a like condition in the whole church. Too often congregants or members assume this disposition, "Let someone else do it." Sometimes we just simply want to show out. This simply means some people won't take the initiative to do anything unless they are asked to do it, paid to do it, or are celebrated for doing it. The purpose thus goes lacking because of these attitudes within the body of Christ. Such a condition is like an automobile with its motor running but its transmission in neutral. It makes a lot of noise and uses a lot of fuel, but it goes nowhere.

The real church of God in Christ is the light of the world. We are like a candle stick. The candle stick's purpose is to "give light unto all that are in the house," Matthew 5:15b that is, to be witnesses of the saving grace of God unto all who are on the inhabited earth. This cannot be done unless there is the fulfillment of duty upon the part of every saved individual, which brings us to the crux of the whole matter.

The scripture teaches the responsibility of every saved

person to unite with the Lord's church to do your part. We must consider our Christian duty. A church can only fulfill its purpose if believers realize and take responsibility in joining themselves to the work of the ministry of Christ. We must put our light on the candlestick where it may shine for the whole world to see as again we are called as the light of the world.

It's easy to sit and become comfortable in the church, touching your saved, sanctified neighbor who looks like you, talks like you, acts like you, dresses like you, dances like you, and the like. However, our light shines best in dark places. We must be willing as the church to be that lighthouse that provides direction, instructions, and guidance, or what I call the "dig." The dig is the things people are needing from the Lord (directions, instructions, and guidance). We must be willing to be a light to those who are in peril until they experience hope.

It is shamefully true that many who have been saved by the grace of God put their light "under a bushel." Oftentimes this is done because we've become ignorant concerning our identity and purpose but deliberate in the escape of our responsibility and accountability. Here are a few excuses and examples that I've heard and seen: A person knows that if he joins a church, they become a contributor to the cause. Much like in your natural households, you assist in the maintaining of the home, cooking, cleaning, doing laundry, paying bills, and the like. It's no different in the church. We are participating members to the greater cause. In other words, a part of that responsibility is ongoing support financially, but herein lies a problem. Some don't want to share in that expense because they don't feel this is a part of their responsibility to care for the house of God.

Haggai 1:4 shares a conversation on this wise with a question, "Why are you living in luxurious houses while my house lies in ruins?" The people of that day didn't feel an urgency to build God's house. They were sedated with their own affairs and lifestyles. They apparently didn't realize verse 6 brings judgment. It says "You have sowed much but have reaped little. You have eaten but don't have enough to become satisfied. You have drunk but don't have enough to be intoxicated. You have clothed yourself but don't have enough to keep warm. And the hired laborer deposits his salary in a bag full of holes."

Now let's look at this twofold, naturally and spiritually. Some people have their homes laid and decked out. They've taken care of the necessities of their homes, but when it comes to God's house, naturally they are not as concerned. Again, this is an avoidance of responsibility, feeling somebody else will handle that. Some feel the church doesn't need their supports financially based on their perceived notion of what the interior and exterior look like. They look at what the preacher is driving and living and decide again that they don't need to assist.

Can I tell you that not all preachers are living off the dollars of members? Some have businesses, jobs, and other means that support their personal necessities. Many handle the contributing support of the members' seed with integrity. The leaders in this category are concerned about the overall well-being of the souls of the people as well as the upkeep of the house of God. Some even take from their own households sacrificially to ensure that

43

nothing is lacking in God's house. Others don't know this because these leaders exemplify integrity and don't share everything they do for God's house to the members. They are not braggadocios giving to be seen, but humbly are led by the Spirit to ensure the members aren't yoked but remain free to serve and worship God without undoing restraints. Now these leaders understand their purpose that they are first partakers and exemplify what the real church of God in Christ should display.

However, the flip side is that some leaders have created a lifestyle of their own off the sacrifices of the people and are not concerned about the overall well-being of their souls at all. These are known as hirelings. A hireling is a person (spiritually speaking) who does what they do (preaching and prophesying using their gifts) purely for a reward or payment. This person leads the people, but not by example. Their motives are selfish and self-centered and are the worst as it relates to their responsibility to care for God's house. They are simply concerned about their own lifestyle and image and will do so at the expense of the people.

This is not a hypercritical statement, but an illustration of a fraction of leaders who fall in this category. When your spiritual lights are cut on you, see through the darkness of form, fashions, and flesh parading in and around the church. Some of these leaders started off doing right, and somewhere and somehow, they go to the left. The pressures and reality of having to hold up the bloodstained banner became too much for some. They started off wanting to please God, which moved to pleasing man and then to pleasing self. Some leaders in this transition developed a sense of entitlement. Others were intoxicated with power. A few felt it was lucrative and provided a lifestyle they've always wanted. However, on the other hand, some felt the pressure was more than they could bear. Their arms became heavy, and they began to feel the warfare. They had mental health issues and just simply became burnt out. Someone might be saying, "This isn't true," but I can only say, "Keep on living, watching, and praying."

Now some have said the preacher lives from the Old Testament, saying Malachi 3 isn't for today's believers. Others feel that we do not need to give because Jesus paid it all.

I agree, and He did, but the work continues though He declared it was finished (not that He was finished, but the work or assignment He was called to do was finished). Leaders who are really called have to get their second wind from the Spirit, so they may stay focused on their true assignment.

Understand that souls are still needing to be saved, healed, and delivered. Backsliders need to be reclaimed, and they need a place to fellowship. Let's keep the oil burning and the light shining. Remember, the Old Testament is the shadow of the New Testament concealed. The New Testament is the Old Testament revealed. Although we don't live in the shadow, the shadow remains revealed when standing in the light or sun/Son. So long as you are hidden in Christ the Son, who is the One who lights up the world, John 8:12 declares, which is one of His great I AMs, "I AM the Light of the world." So, whenever you move under/in the Son, so does your shadow.

Listen, your supports aren't just needed in the area of your finances. The work in/of the ministry encompasses your time, talent, and treasures, which are all needed as the real church of God in Christ. We must get people back to the spirit of the matter, so they won't lose sight or heart on their purpose as a member of the body of Christ. Now there is one body with many members. Our diversity makes us unique in how we function in our purpose.

Psalm 133:1–3 provides the beauty of unity, "Behold how good and pleasant it is for brethren to dwell together in unity."

1. It's like precious ointment that flowed from the head, to the beard even to the skirts.
2. As the dew of Harmon and as the dew that descended upon the mountains of Zion
3. For there the Lord commanded the blessing even life forever more.

The benefits of our unification stand the test of time, for where there is unity, there is strength. Now I love the fact that our difference will make a difference as the real church of God in Christ.

Being unique and different comes at a cost/price. We don't live to "get in where we fit in." We are the *ekklesia*, a people who were called out to stand up and out. Do you know who you are? Well, let me give this quick sidebar reminder:

- "You—are a chosen generation; a royal priesthood, a holy nation, a peculiar people." (1 Peter 2:9)
- "You are made the righteousness of God in Christ." (2 Corinthians 5:21)

- "You are more than a conquer." (Romans 8:37)
- "I know the thoughts I think towards you said the Lord, thoughts to prosper you, to give you a future and a hope." (Jeremiah 29:11)
- "You are blessed in the city and the field." (Deuteronomy 28:3)
- "You are the head and NOT the tail, above ONLY and not beneath." (Deuteronomy 28:13)

So, when you know who God says you are, you'll realize that you are that living organism and that you can give hope to anyone you touch. So, the operations of organizations and denominations are essential structures that should act as assistance in the building and maintaining of the foundational stone from which we stand. Proverbs 11:3 reads, "If the foundations be destroyed what can the righteous do?" However, these are in no means the final authority; nor can they be as it relates to our purpose as the people of God.

Too often people are introduced and become connected to structural undertakings of such, but find themselves unfortunately stuck and entangled (snared, entrapped, and caught up) in these mere human organizations and denominations, but are not often progressive when wrong perceptions and the traditions of men become the base and not Christ. It remains that the traditions of men make the word of God of non-effect. Unfortunately, we see people becoming more loyal to what is constructed and conducive by the arm of flesh than that which is destined by the Spirit.

CHAPTER 9

Where Your Trust Goes, the Power Flows

Listen, we must keep our trust and refuge in God, first and foremost. The Bible encourages us not to trust in our flesh or the flesh of others. Here's why.

Jeremiah 17:5 says, "Cursed is a man who puts his/her trust in man and makes (continually) them their strength turning their hearts away from the Lord." Psalm 20:7 tells us, "Some trust in chariots and horses, but we will trust in God." Proverbs 19:21 reminds us, "There are many plans in the heart of man, but it is the Lord's purpose that will prevail."

Psalm 73:26 says, "Our flesh and heart may fail, but God is the strength of my heart and my portion forever." Psalm 127:1 declares, "Unless the LORD builds the house, its builders labor uselessly. Unless the LORD guards the city, its security forces keep watch uselessly." Psalm 146:3–4 reads, "Do not look to nobles, nor to mere human beings who cannot save. when they stop breathing, they return to the ground: on that very day their plans evaporate!"

Proverbs 16:9 tells us, "A man's heart plans his way, but the Lord guides (continually) his steps." Proverbs 28:26a says, "He that trusts (continually) in his own heart is a fool." And Romans 8:8 states, "Those who are in the realm of the flesh cannot please God."

What encouraging scriptures to tell us why we shouldn't place our trust in the arm of flesh, ours or anyone else's. Remember, we are finite, but Jesus is infinite (eternal, immutable, and unchanging). Simply put, He is absolute!

Now don't get me wrong; hear me in the Spirit. Every undertaking needs structural conductors that are led by the Spirit to carry out the tasks, so we won't step out of our place in grace assuming we know what's best. We must never forget we are not the owners of the people, plans, or purposes, but managing conservators through the will of God through his Son Jesus by faith.

When the real church of God in Christ is really being directed by the Spirit, we will remain grounded on the foundation of love on how to lead the people as Jesus wills, not how we will. Now it is certainly true that these human organizations and denominations can and often perform good works in their functioning, but we must be reminded that all the glory belongs to God. "For it is God who works in us to will and to act in order to fulfill his good purpose" (Philippians 2:13).

So, we know our purpose of the real church of God in Christ is grounded in the founder, ruler, and overseer that is far above every other earthly authority, power dominion, and name that was, that is, and that will ever be (past, present, and future).

Ephesians 3:21 concurs, "To him be glory in the church and in the Messiah Jesus to all generations forever! Amen." If there is any other belief or idea though that thinks otherwise, they are deceiving themselves.

As the real church of God in Christ, we shine like glowing embers that set ablaze the hearts of those who truly live by precept and example of its author. God's people are called to be faithfully committed to the cause. 1 Corinthians 4:2 says, "Moreover it is required in stewards that a man/woman be found faithful." I reiterate to you that it's not what we say. It's what we do that speaks to our representation as the real church of God in Christ.

CHAPTER 10

How Are You Living?

It's not how we live when we are only in the company of believers. Can I tell you that there are many whom I would call two-faced? In other words, a two-faced person would smile in your face but stab you in the back. They will pretend to have your best interests at heart, but all the while when they are scandalous out of sight. This is not becoming of the real church of God in Christ. In 1 Corinthians 3: 1 – 3 Apostle Paul told the church at Corinth, "Brothers, I couldn't talk to you as spiritual people but as worldly people, as mere infants in the Messiah. I gave you milk to drink, not solid food, because you weren't ready for it! That's because you are still worldly. As long as there is jealousy and quarreling among you, you are worldly and living by human standards, aren't you?" In other words, the Apostle was sharing the state of the condition of the church's immaturity. He ended his thought staying, "These things ought NOT be named among you."

Listen, I know I haven't always got it right, and I'm sure I am not to only one who has witnessed or had to oftentimes make my flesh take a back seat to allow the Spirit to speak forth. Many times, I had the opportunity (rightfully so) to get in my flesh, but I made a choice not to allow my flesh to be in control that could cause someone to stumble or lose their appetite for the presence of God. Truthfully, I've fussed, got upset in my flesh, and had a few tantrums. I've asked God, "Why did I have to apologize when that person wronged me?" However, God began to continue to work on me, chiseling and cutting away the overgrowth until I came to a place called "I surrender."

See, oftentimes we don't want to be transparent because we hold titles and positions and have influence with the people. We don't want the people to know that if you pinch me, I will say "ouch" too. Let me tell you. Sometimes I get beside myself, and my flesh must be brought back into subjection. But like David, I cried out for help.

Have I failed in making the right choices every time? Yes, I have! I believe when we as leaders start being transparent and not translucent, the people will also take ownership of their wrongs. What's the difference? Transparency is when light goes through undisturbed without distorting, thus making an image. Translucent allows light through but doesn't produce an image because it is frosted. My God today!

But can I tell you that I thank God for the Holy Ghost who lights a fire on the inside and quickens me when I am wrong? You see, some people get upset when they are convicted, but I am happy that God sees all, knows all, and loves us enough to correct us. We know Hebrews 12:6 says, "Don't lose heart when the Lord rebukes you; He disciplines the ones he loves." If we don't take to God's corrections, we are not legitimate (true sons and daughters). I know this may be hard saying to someone, but no good parent will sit by and do nothing when they see their child in error or danger.

Therefore, your lifestyle must line up with the word and

confession as a believer. Understand people are watching your life up close and personal as well as far off. They are just waiting for your fall to prove a point, much like what Jesus experienced with the religious sect (to point a finger back at him).

You remember the woman who was caught in the very act of adultery in John 8:1–11. This woman was brought before her accusers, but not the man. I don't have the time to deal with that part. The Pharisees told Jesus the woman was caught in the act of adultery. Now, these Pharisees said to Jesus in verse 5, "Moses said to stone her" (pulling from the Old Testament Deuteronomy 22:22–25). Then you see their motive with the presented question: What say you? Remember, this wasn't because they wanted to reveal the sin of the woman only, but these religious mindsets had an agenda with the intention of entrapping Jesus in His response to catch Him in a snare.

Jesus replied, "He who is without sin cast the first stone." From the eldest to the youngest, they dropped their stones and walked away. I said that to say this: some people think the church is judgmental and unfair. This is constituted by their encounters with religious mindsets that have ulterior motives. This kind pushes people back, bringing them into bondage as if they have it all together, never messing up. Romans 3:23 reminds us, "All have sinned and come short of God's glory."

We can't forget our own testimonies. Remember, some of these people may never enter what we call the church building, but they will look at our lives and judge the collective body of Christ. They will see the actions of one and think that this is how the real church of God in Christ is when, on the contrary, that individual may simply be representing themselves, but the church feels the backlash of such behaviors.

Jesus is seen throughout the scriptures teaching personal responsibility, reminding us that we are set apart for His use. In this, our lives and lifestyles should represent or re-present His church as we are the church bodily.

CHAPTER 11

Be the Light

Jesus says, "Let your light so shine before men, that they may see your good works, and glorify your Father which is in heaven" (Matthew 5:16). I know we've covered this, but repetition is a good teacher.

The word in the above text that gives the greatest force and fire is a term often overlooked because of its seeming insignificance. It is the little word "so." This word, *houtos*, in the Greek is often translated "on this wise" (Matthew 1:18), "thus" (Matthew 2:5), "after this manner" (Matthew 6:9), "on this fashion" (Mark 2:12), and "in this manner" (Revelation 11:5). It is an adverb, and it defines how or where the action is to be performed. In other words, this is not presented as an afterthought, but a continuation of the action that is breaking forth. In Matthew 5:16, it shows where the light is to shine, for the reference is to the candlestick in verse 15. It is to shine "in this manner," upon the candlestick.

"Let your light of witness shine from the candle stand of the church." This cannot mean anything else than that the Lord's disciples have a duty to unite with His church, shining bright and therein glorifying God.

The New Testament example and teaching are clear on this matter, as we see from the literal rendering of Acts 2:47, "And the Lord was adding to the church daily those that were being saved." The Lord adds to the church. He brings salvation to the lost. In John 14:6, Jesus declares himself in another I AM. "I AM the way, and the truth and the life no one can come to the Father except through him." In the real church of God in Christ, it has drawing power. The church as we know it is evolving/ changing, though the base from which it stands is solid as a rock.

Interchangeably as we engage in the working of the ministry, people come and go from church to church from time to time. Sadly, in these last days, there are multitudes of "non-believers as well as believers" who are members of nobody's church. This is more common in the people who have a vast amount of options where they can watch Christian-based shows, broadcasts, podcasts, and the like from the touch of their fingers in the comfort of their own homes. This has a grave effect on the local churches who were designed to bring personal touches to the people. However, many today prefer to use untouchable methods and are content with what church used to be like and sometimes indifferent to what really is developing to today. We understand Hebrews 10:25 says, "Don't neglect meeting together as is the habit of some but encouraging one another even more as you see the day of the Lord coming nearer."

Some in this latter day take a different meaning to this text and do what we've just mentioned: chillaxing in their homes and watching church from the multimedia streams that technology affords us in the land today.

CHAPTER 12

The Power of Touch

However, the disservice to this action is that you may get a feel and thrill and then shout and dance, but you can't strengthen a person you can't touch. Give me a moment to deal with the power of touch.

The real church of God in Christ operates as its chief operating officer, Jesus. Jesus had a touchable priesthood. In other words, He is touch with the feelings of our infirmities but moved by our faith. Our faith is full action in the house.

We through faith in Him are a mobile crisis and recovery unit, in many cases, spiritual first responders with the ability to touch the hearts of people in this world on this journey in Christendom. Jesus modeled the way, showing us as the real church of God in Christ how to use the power of touch. Let's take a moment to look at some people who were impacted, changed, healed, and delivered by the power of His touch.

In Matthew 8:4, Jesus encounters a leper, a person who had a skin condition. This leper fell down and worshipped Jesus, asking if He could heal and make him clean. Verse 3 demonstrates the power of touch when Jesus stretched out his hand and said, "I will; be thou clean." This leper was immediately cleansed. There are several points to notice in this passage:

1. Jesus walked amongst the people. As believers, we mustn't be afraid to walk among those who have been considered outcasts because they have issues, problems, and conditions.

2. Jesus was moved with compassion. As believers, we mustn't shut up our bowels of compassion when we see a need.

3. Jesus listened to his request. As believers, we mustn't be so removed from hearing what is being spoken naturally and spiritually. Jesus heard what the request was and granted it. Apostle Paul again, while in prison, heard a man from Macedonia crying out in prayer for help in a vision, and he responded (Acts 16:9).

Jesus's walk among the people, compassion, and active listening led him to respond, which provided immediate results. It wasn't just this leper Jesus healed through the vehicle of touch. Jesus touched Peter's mother-in-law in Mark 1:30–3.

He touched a young girl in Mark 5:41–42. He touched blind men in Matthew 9:29–30. He touched a man who was mute in Mark 7:32–25. While in the garden, upon Peter cutting off High Priest Malchus' right ear, Jesus destroyed the evidence via touch. What a mighty God we serve! Can I tell you not only did Jesus touch the people, the people touched Him and received healing?

The woman with the issue of blood in Luke 8:43–44 touched the hem in the Him. My God today, she was healed. Many people who pressed upon Him in Mark 3:9–10, 5:29–30 were healed, and many more times the people by faith touched Jesus and received their healing. Not only did this happen with Jesus, but with the apostle. In Acts 5:15, although it doesn't say that Peter's shadow healed people, verse 16 says that all the people were healed. Now again, whether it was by his shadow or just his very presence, it left a lasting impact. Apostle Paul laid hands upon the disciples in Acts 19:6. They were filled with the Holy Ghost, spoke in tongues, and prophesied.

In that same text around verses 11–12, we see how God demonstrated miracles through apostle Paul. Those who were diseased and had evil spirit also were healed by handkerchiefs and aprons that had touched the apostle's skin.

When people see the church in demonstration of the power, people will come by the drawing of the Lord, and the church will begin to grow by leaps and bounds? When there is noise that Jesus is in the midst, there will be demonstration and manifestation of His power.

CHAPTER 13

Member, Fellowship, and Relationship

Now let me clear this up. Please know that church membership, while not necessary to salvation, is certainly necessary to the development and growth as a believer. You see, when we come together, we can glean from one another. In other words, what you may be going through, someone else can bring encouragement because they just came out of that very thing. We're not called to just be on the roll in membership, but as believers in fellowship. This is the "Koinonia" joint participation. As believers working in this kingdom vineyard, we must be helpers together in the work, purpose, and our fellowship with one another.

1 Corinthians 1:9–10 reads, "Faithful is the God by whom you were called into fellowship with his Son Jesus the Messiah, our Lord." The real church of God in Christ understands and recognizes that all three of these (the working, the purpose of fellowship, and relationship) work together for the edifying of the body of Christ. In fellowship, we develop relationships. We understand according to 1 Corinthians 6:020 that we have a duty to respond wholeheartedly to what we were given. The scripture declares that we are "bought with a price: therefore, glorify God in your body, and in your spirit, which are God's."

In this, it shows the instrument wherewith to glorify God is our bodies and spirit that will bring change to our souls. Our bodies are the temple of the Holy Ghost (v. 19), the vehicle wherein we house the soul and spirit. Our soul is our desires (what we want), our intellect (what we think), and our emotions (what we feel). Can I tell you that the acronym to them all spells the word "die"? We must die to our desires, intellects, and emotions and yield to the fact that we were (past tense), are (presence tense), and will be (future tense) benefactors of the ultimate payment Jesus gave for the redemption and propitiation of our sins.

We must give our whole hearts (spirit) unto the Lord. Our spirit is what was made in the image and likeness of God according to Genesis 1:26–27. This wasn't so we could just have the look, but that we may know that as the expressed image of God, we also have His creativity to declare, decree, and "work the works of Him who have called us out of darkness into His marvelous light" (1 Peter 2:9).

Ephesians 3:21 shows the place to reveal His glory, in the church (us). We are the church of the living God bodily. So let's glorify Him. As the real church of God in Christ, we understand that everyone in their natural state is in darkness. King David declared in Psalms 51.5 "Behold, I was shapen in iniquity; and in sin did my mother conceive me." David though he was a king understood his state, condition and limitations. He knew that God and only God can enlighten him according to Psalm 18:28, "For thou wilt light my candle: the Lord my God will enlighten my darkness." No candle was ever lit by an external fire, for it is lifeless and cold until the internal flame is applied to it. So, neither can a man light their own spiritual candle. Again, only God can give eternal life.

However, once this candle is lit, what then? Immediately this individual is brought under another obligation, to put their light of testimony on the candlestick as the church and let it shine before men that God may be glorified.

No one is faithful to their responsibility until they allow God's light to shine through them, reflecting their image. So in this, we know that no human corporation, organization or denomination, reformation, cult, or religious group can compare or compete with the truth and authenticity of Lord's church.

Satan often tells lies, attempting to make incompetent the "house of God, which is the church of the living God, the pillar and ground of the truth" (1 Timothy 3:15). However, once again, no person, place, or thing above, beneath, and around can stop the fire that burns from within presented and the light that shines without, as found in the real church of God in Christ for they understand "the entrance of His word giveth light" (Psalm 119:30). Can I encourage you to stay LIT (love ignites truth).

When you're ignited, you will continue in the movement, purpose, and work of God. You will become fishers of men as Jesus denoted and modeled before the disciples.

CHAPTER 14

Evangelism

Now understand that many parts connect to bring about the most important mission of the real church of God in Christ, evangelism. We've covered much of this, discussing the Great Commission, where they are working and functioning one in the same.

However, in the last verse of Matthew 28, Jesus encourages and says to His disciples according to the Living Bible, "Therefore go and make disciples in all the nations, baptizing them into the name of the Father, and of the Son and of the Holy Spirit and then teach these new disciples to obey all the commands I have given you; and be sure of this—that I am with you always, even to the end of the world." This is the crux of what we should be all about as the people of God. It is the meat of the matter.

We understand that our assignment is to go to the hedges, highways, byways, airways, and alleyways, right where the people are. Then we are truly evangelizing, bringing hope and making disciples with the good news of the gospel of Jesus Christ.

In making disciples as the real church of God in Christ according to scripture, we must do it orderly. Everything should be done decently and in order. One means to function in this order is apostolically.

CHAPTER 15

Apostolic Order

The apostolic order and function of the real church of God in Christ can be seen in the functional purpose or spiritual governmental structure of the apostles in the New Testament church. The word "missionary" comes from a Latin word meaning the same as the Greek word *Apostolos*, or "one sent forth." The apostle Paul wrote much of the New Testament, which outlines the functions of the fivefold or God-called ministry (apostle, prophet, evangelist, pastor, and teacher), according to Ephesians 4:11–13. Each of these offices has a specific function, which we will discuss. However, it is necessary to understand the apostolic order as seen through the scripture. First, let's examine six critical functions of the apostles from apostle Paul's revelatory perception.

1. **Taking the gospel to unreached areas**. Apostle Paul said to the Romans, "It has always been his ambition to preach the gospel where Christ was not known, so that he would not be building on someone else's foundation" (Romans 15:20). In other words, the apostle is saying in this big world there yet remains a vast amount of people who haven't heard the good news. Apostle Paul felt it necessary to reach this target population. An apostle

will identify and establish areas for us to reach with the good news.

2. **Laying a firm foundation (Christ Himself) for the churches being established.** Apostle Paul speaks of this important apostolic role, "By the grace God has given me, I laid a foundation as a wise master builder, and someone else is building on it. But each one should be careful how he builds. For no one can lay any foundation other than the one already laid, which is Jesus Christ" (1 Corinthians 3:10–11). The apostle is speaking from his experience and call, providing a warning to those who would share in the building up of God's kingdom. The apostle says the foundation that he builds upon himself is Christ. He speaks to the truth that we should be careful how we build. In other words, as corporations, organizations, denominations, and the like, we can't forget that it is upon Christ, as the songwriter Edward Mote (1837), reminded us that "My Hope is Built on Nothing Less." This song rings volumes when you know that Jesus is our final authority all other ground is like quicksand.

3. **Training the initial leaders and appointing elders.** When Paul and Barnabas made their second visit to Lystra, Iconium, and Pisidian Antioch, they preached, prayed, fasted, strengthened, and encouraged the new converts (disciples) to continue in the faith. This conversion came with a warning that trying times will come, but they understood it would take many to advance

the kingdom agenda. Therefore, they ordained elders in each church (Acts 14:21–23). Paul likewise instructs Titus to "set in order" the churches in Crete. To set in order was to increase in laborers by positioning them to the work and purpose for which we were called. The apostles then encouraged them to endure, to go through these hardships that will come with the advancement that they may enter the kingdom of God. Paul and Titus appointed elders in every church/city (Titus 1:5). Apostle Paul understood the work or furtherance of the kingdom requires efforts on everyone's part. He understood that although he was considered a master builder, he wasn't the end-all or be-all and certainly couldn't do the work all by himself.

4. **Dealing with specific problems, false doctrines, or sins in the churches that had been occurring**. Paul's first letter to the Corinthians illustrates his use of his apostolic authority to speak to the issues and problems in the church he had planted at Corinth, including disunity, immaturity, pride, immorality, taking other believers to court before secular authorities, questions about celibacy and marriage, disputes about meat sacrificed to idols, wrong handling of the Lord's Supper, misuse of spiritual gifts, confusion about the resurrection, and so forth. The apostle knew that though he was incarcerated, if he didn't deal with these issues, they would continue to fester, bringing dissension in the church, which would affect the growth of the body of Christ. Paul was influential even

from the prison walls. He took action to bring correction in the spirit of love.

5. **Promoting unity in the body of Christ**. The unity concept is applied on many different levels. In the church of Philippi (Philippians 4:2), Paul had to deal with a situation of contention between two ladies in the local assembly, Euodia and Syntyche. The apostle revealed his apostolic voice, encouraging the ladies to "be of the same mind in the Lord." In the church of Corinth (1 Corinthians 3:4), there was apparently citywide disunity in the church because of various believers choosing to rally around dynamic leaders such as Paul and Apollos. Paul, in this text, also performed the apostolic role of rebuking while yet providing a comparable focus that it's not of them, but of God. He reminded them they were only servants in whom they believed the good news, but the Lord causes the seed to grow. In this, the apostle brought the people back to God.

6. **Demonstrating and imparting the supernatural dimension of the kingdom of God**. Although it is God's intention for all believers to heal the sick, cast out demons, and perform miracles by the power of the Holy Spirit, those in apostolic ministry are particularly to bear this credential. Thus, it is said that "God did extraordinary miracles through Paul" (Acts 19:11). Apostles were often used in a special way to impart and identify the gifts and power of God in other believers. They helped in the cultivation of those gifts, stirring up the believers.

Affirming these six expressed purposes of the apostles in the first-century church, it must be realized that each of the apostles in the New Testament was unique as to how he carried out his apostolic role. We are uniquely designed with the fingerprint of God for the workings we are called to do. We may have the same scripture but express the revelatory production totally differently.

When I was in college, we had what was before then and even now what is known as major and minors of studies. This means we had a specific specialty course and then the general one. For example, I majored in social work but minored in mental health. They work together for the overall working of what I was called to do in the secular sector. It is the same in the spiritual arena as well. You can major in one gift and minor in another likewise in an office.

Although Peter was in the office of an apostle, he particularly was gifted in reaching out to the lost (evangelism). In other words, he displayed the minor of what is not least but a part of his full ministry. Timothy was a pastor, yet apostle Paul encouraged him to do the work of the evangelist. Paul seemed to excel in teaching and building believers together as a functional expression of the body of Christ in his apostolic role.

John's apostleship carried with it a prophetic heart that God's people would continually walk together in righteousness with the Lord and love each other. James, the half-brother of Jesus, also seems to have functioned as an apostle, even though the focus of his ministry was more pastoral and localized in Jerusalem. It is also important to realize that having an apostolic calling did not automatically mean that the apostle had the right to exercise full authority in all places and situations.

It was a ministry based upon relationship and not only on calling. Also it means that the authority of an apostle diminished in certain ways once the local church was firmly established and provided with the oversight of local elders.

The relationship and authority still existed when necessary to intervene in problems not being remedied by the local leadership, but it was Paul's perspective that he was like a father whose role of authority diminished once his son or daughter reached adulthood. His heart was not to establish a "chain of command," but rather to see each church established under the headship of Christ.

Under the headship of Christ, the real church of God in Christ understands the order of God. They walk under the mantle and guidance of the Holy Spirit with their sole purpose of continuing the work and purpose in which the early church began and continues. Their vision is to reach the unreached areas as well as those closest. It is the Lord's will that no one be lost. We as the real church of God in Christ should have this mentality when dealing with people near and abroad.

However, although the gospel has gone out to some degree to every nation of the earth through the vehicle of technology, there is still an undetermined amount of people of various remote, geographically or linguistically, isolated areas that have never even heard the good news.

We are fortunate to have technological advances, but we must get these advancements to unreached areas that does not have them so the world at large could be inundated with the hope that is found in Jesus the Christ, our Lord.

Let take a moment to look at world evangelism statistics. There are approximately almost 7 billion people on this planet. In a world where people are entering and exiting just as fast, these statistics sound the alarm and warrant action for believers:

- Births per minute: 266
- Deaths per minute: 108
- Population of unreached people groups (billions): 2.84[2]
- Largest countries (in millions): China (1,346), India (1,241), United States (312), Indonesia (238), and Brazil (197)
- Major religions: Christians (2.3 billion), Muslims (1.6 billion), Hindus (952 million), Buddhist (468 million), Chinese folk-religionist (458 million), ethnoreligionist (269 million), and nonreligious (658 million)
- Major traditional branches of Christianity: Roman Catholics (1.2 billion), Protestants (426 million), Independents (378 million), Orthodox (271 million), and Anglicans (88 million)
- Christians by continent: Africa (475 million), Asia (354 million), Europe (559 million), Latin America (543 million), North America (231 million), and Oceania (24 million)

What does this all mean? Although various statistical facts are yet rapidly coming to surface, there are also approximately

74,000 people across the globe who come to faith in Christ, which is approximately 3,083 believers every hour of every day. Still over 3 billion people in the world are unreached.

The Joshua Project provides interesting statistics that warrant a look. Sixty-seven countries are represented in the 10/40 window worldwide. However, he reports five out of six people group in the 10/40 window are unreached. All hands are needed on deck. The work continues. The above statistics can be found by going to https://joshuaproject.net/assets/media/handouts/status-of-world-evangelization.pdf

Now, we are not oblivious to the fact that there are additives to what the origination of Christianity means. We know that various sects have throughout time tried to dissect and redirect the founder and foundation, but as believers, we cannot afford to sit back and do nothing. We can't afford to lose our hearts or focus. We must act now!

We must yet choose Jesus Christ and work His missions His way so global outreach/evangelism/missions can continue as we as the real church of God in Christ can reach out with the good news. The real church of God in Christ is like fire lighting up the world but listen. It takes money, contributions, supports, and prayers to assist in this overall mission. Matthew 24:14 tells us "And this Gospel of the kingdom will be proclaimed throughout the world as a testimony to all nations, and then the end will come."

Know that we are blessed to be a blessing. Luke 6:38 encourages us to "give and it shall come back to you good measure, pressed-down, shaken together and running over shall men give unto your bosom." It's more blessed to give than to receive.

Look at what apostle Paul encourages us to do in 2 Corinthians 9:8–11. Besides, God is able to make every blessing of yours overflow for you so that in every situation you will always have all you need for any good work. Verse 9–11 says,

> He scatters everywhere and gives to the poor; his righteousness lasts forever, now he who supplies seed to the farmer and bread to eat will also supply you with seed and multiply it and enlarge the harvest that results from your righteousness in every way you will grow richer and become even more generous, and this will cause other to give thanks to God because of us.

The apostle declares a prophetic blessing upon the people who keep their hands open, and their bowels of compassion open toward the work of the ministry of God in Christ.

Apostle Paul shared with us the necessary action steps that need to be performed. The apostles understood the foundational scripture in Ephesians 2: 20 – 22 that states "And are built upon the foundation of the apostles and prophets, Jesus Christ himself being the chief corner stone; In whom all the building fitly framed together growth unto an holy temple in the Lord: In whom ye also are builded together for an habitation of God through the Spirit."

When any religious group, organization, denomination, or

independent contractors attempt to lay a foundation without the cornerstone, we find that many can't maintain or sustain. Colossians 2:8 resounds this louder, telling us, "See to it that no one takes you captive through hollow and deceptive philosophy, which depends on human traditions and the elemental spiritual forces of this world rather than on Christ." I come back to my favorite hymnal, "My hope is built on nothing less than Jesus blood and righteousness" (Edward Mote, 1837).

Another part that can't be overlooked is the training of leaders. Today seminaries and Bible schools have largely replaced the apostolic function of training leaders.

Now don't misunderstand me. I believe that the people of God ought to "study to show themselves unto God," according to 2 Timothy 2:15. It may be that the mode of transport to understand biblical principles may come because of attending a Bible school or seminary. Now with the advancement of technology, it is thus shifting where you can get biblical knowledge by the touch of your finger. However, the means and mode aren't a replacement of apostolic order.

Unfortunately, today the order in which God has outlined things has shifted. There was a time when the real church of God in Christ adhered to the precept, example, and structure of the apostolic order. The apostles in times past would lay hands according to God's will. Now the appointing of leaders of local churches has been made a matter of congregational voting in some of the reformations. These leaders are now selected by a denominational hierarchy or ambitious, aspiring young preachers simply starting their own churches appointing themselves as pastors, prophets, apostles, and the like.

It's no doubt that many of these leaders are called, but they are not often prepared to assume these places of great responsibility. When God calls you, He also in turn equipped you for that call. So although people are studious in their studies, they may have been good students at the seminary, ministries, training centers, and so forth, but they are likely to miss the kind of personal training and character development that comes from God alone. Now I know there are those such as apostle Paul, who mentored Timothy, Elijah to Elisha, Moses to Joshua, and so forth, but the truth remains. If you are not grounded in character, your giftings won't sustain you.

I believe it was Bishop T.D. Jakes who said on Twitter in 2015, "Your gift will carry you where your character can't keep you." What an awesome revelatory word to help keep us grounded so we won't bring infractions in the body. As we know, "hurt people hurt others." Therefore, we need the oversight of those who have more insight, hindsight, and foresight to present problems of yesterday and today.

Another need for the continuation of God's apostolic order is problem-solving. Local churches frequently encounter problems that they have difficulty solving without assistance. Some pastors and leaders are frequently without any personal accountability and often have no one to give them input regarding church problems. Sometimes local leaders have blind spots that also prohibit them from seeing even their own shortcomings that exist. There is still a need today for men of apostolic authority to pierce through the blindness, ignorance, and pride, speaking the word of God to areas of sin, imbalance, false doctrine, division, and other problems that are ever increasing. The apostolic order deals the unity and connective-ness of the church.

According to John 17:1, Jesus states, "Father make them one as we are one." The disunity of the body of Christ is like a foreign substance that presents as clean and pure but is not. Wrong motives and intentions are the underlining factors.

Understand that disunity (disconnection) is scandalous. It robs us as the real church of God in Christ of the full blessing of God and weakens our testimony to the lost. Men of genuine apostolic hearts have a burden to see God's people come together as a united family and army. They're able to see an overview of the universal church around the world and can sense the heartbeat of what the Lord is speaking. Vision defined is the ability to think about and plan the future with wisdom. Everyone has a vision and rightfully so, but where is God's vision?

God tells Habakkuk in verse 2:2, "Write (do something) down the revelations/vision and make it plain on tables (which is our hearts) so that the runner can carry the correct message to others." Unfortunately, the message often gets lost in translation but is sorely needed in the church today. Only men and women of apostolic insight and authority can bring it about in a significant way.

Lastly, apostolic order understands the season, timing, and the hour as never before to demonstrate the power of God. Ecclesiastes 3:1 says, "To everything there is a season, and a time to every purpose under the heaven." Understand that it only takes two to believe in agreement in order to operate in the miracles of God because Jesus will be in the midst. Matthew 18:20 reminds us, "Where two or three are gather in his name he will be in the midst," but He won't do anything until we do what Matthew 18:19 says, "I also tell you this: if two of you agree here on earth concerning anything you ask, my Father in heaven will do it for you." When we simply believe, power for change follows.

Mark 16:17 reads, "And these signs shall follow them that believe … In my name shall they cast out devils, they shall speak with new tongues, if they take up any deadly thing, it shall not hurt them, they shall lay hands on the sick and they shall recover." See, we live in a day when God is moving mightily to restore signs and wonders to the church.

Too long we have relied upon our intellect, human wisdom, and persuasive words, the very things Paul put no confidence in, "My message and my preaching were not in wise and persuasive words, but with demonstration of the Spirit's power, so that your faith might not rest on men's wisdom, but on God's power" (1 Corinthians 2:4–5). Psalm 62:11 concurs and concludes, "God hath spoken once and twice have I heard this, POWER belongs to God."

CHAPTER 16

The Power of the Church

A flashback from then to now takes us on a journeying of the presence of the power of God activated in the real church of God in Christ. Know that this power wasn't isolated or can be monopolized upon by any one organization, denomination, or reformation. As we know, various nationalities of churches alike were and still are known and respected in many ways for their organizational hierarchy, from the Southern Baptist, Full Baptist, and Charismatic to the Pentecostal pop, drop, and lock, which displayed a captivating expression to it often being recognized as what is mostly known to be the church in the eyes of some.

Much of the charismatic operational background in the African American church settings represented what was or is internationally known as the movement and power seen in the church. The Azusa Street outpouring started in 1906 in a former livery stable at 312 Azusa Street, Los Angeles. A handful of believers under the leadership of an African American Holiness preacher named William J. Seymour (1880–1922) would be the conductor, if you will, of this remarkable beginning of power displayed in this reformation and that which what was to come. During the 1906 Azusa wave, many experienced the outpouring in baptism of the Holy Spirit in the lives of various denominational compositions, where many were filled with the evidence of speaking in tongues as demonstrated in Acts 1–2. Acts 1:8 says, "But ye shall receive power after that the Holy Ghost is come upon you, and ye shall be witnesses unto me both in Jerusalem, in all Judea, and in Samaria, and unto the utter most part of the earth."

Regrettably, a gross misinterpretation of the scripture here shifted the very purpose of the power. Oftentimes people read the scriptures and don't study, which leads to misinterpretation and misrepresentation of the intent and content of the text. The very purpose of Holy Ghost power was not just given so we could speak in tongues, dance, and shout. The power was given to work in conjunction with what Matthew 28 declares to be the Great Commission.

The key words declared in Acts 1:8 eludes to the work that we are to be witnesses. Unfortunately, some churches and ministries have forgotten the mission is again to go. Go do what? Tell men, women, boys, and girls everywhere of every nation that Jesus saves. As the real church of God in Christ, this is what we do because this is who we are! Understand that everything ties together for the overall working of kingdom building of souls. When we build the people, the people will build the buildings. A building is necessary, so we can fellowship together. However, we come in the building to get strength and encouragement to go out where the vast amount of people is. We're not to get comfortable inside and forget the power we must reach out.

Now reaching out, we as the people of God should have the same mindset as Jesus, who said in John 4:34, "My meat (food, substance and nourishment) is to DO the WILL of him who sent me and to finish his WORK." The Bible, our final authority, reveals many situations, circumstances, and characters that provide an inside view of the do's and the don'ts on this Christian journey. We understand that through the mindsets of that day up to this present day, some people have expressed, "Forms of godliness but denied the power there of" (2 Timothy 3:5). Their forms acted as symbols, which only represented an outward manifestation of human perception without an inside change.

The symbols of the church are aligned with some of the symbols that are visible and recognizable in the church of yesterday and today, such as crosses, steeples, bells, statues, and pictures of former and current leaders. Now there is a more reflective presence on the scene. The crosses used to be on the church; now they are in the pockets of bishops, elders, and apostles. Fancy and blinged-out robes, suits, and dresses are the latest in pulpiteer attire. There was a time when robes were used to hide the outer appearance of the preacher-man/woman, so the people would not get fixated on the preacher's outer wear and be distracted from the message. Nowadays, for the most part, it is for show and style. From the sleek colorful cassock to the clergy collars, many outward things seem to have replaced the humility of some of the twenty-first century leaders.

There was a time when the leader/preacher only wore their wedding ring. Now it's almost to the point that you can't hear the message from the glitz and glam of their stunning diamonds to the bishopric rocks.

Here's another transparent moment. Let me interject this. Once I attended a "home-going service" of a man of God. There was a section roped off for all the preachers, clergy, ministers, and so on. However, it was amazing to see so many people who was just a layperson with clergy collars on. I was asked by another minister (who had the same mindset of "giving honor where honor was due," just wanting to pay respect to the passing man of god). We asked each other, "Were they passing out collars at the door?"

I am quite amazed at the fact that people who were just laypersons are now referred as minister, bishop, evangelist, prophet, doctors, and so forth. They hadn't been saved but a minute. You call yourself bishop and the like, and you are barely over the drinking age. Some have gotten so caught up on the outward appearance of what they think the real church of God in Christ should be that the power of being important has become intoxicating.

I thought to myself, *Wow!* I began to pray because the church has lost its focus and real vision. We continue to misrepresent our God because:

- We have become more excited about a personality instead of the real anointing. I'm talking about the anointing (the expressed power of God) that destroys yokes and removes burdens according to Isaiah 10:27.
- We have settled for programs and musicals and not progression of the mission.
- We have become more excited about entertaining folks (lights, camera, and action) than seeing lives changed through the taught word and power of God.

I remember the guest minister who was called to share with

the people set himself in a higher seat, making a statement of what I consider foul and distasteful. He called the people what no leader should even utter out their mouths concerning the people of God simply because he didn't get the response he was seeking.

In this, his reply was demeaning and derogatory, speaking as if the people were beneath him. I thought once again, *how offensive this is to the people and God.* Please don't misunderstand me. I believe that, had he been sensitive to the Spirit, he would've, could've, and should've been mindful of who he was referring to (the chosen people of God). The Holy Spirit knows God's will and mind. The Holy Spirit brings conviction to our hearts when we get out of line. However, there are leaders or those who are in leadership positions who have taken their influence to super-rule the people. Not all, but some people in influential roles have become driven with the power and not led by the Spirit treating the people as precious cargo.

When we forget that power belongs to God and that we are mere conduits that allow ourselves to be guided by the Spirit when interacting with the people, we can cause wreckage and offenses to occur. Some people are often wounded and walk in the spirit of offense because of the failure of men and women of the cloth who forget who is really in charge. Tactlessly, these kinds of leaders have become desensitized to the heart of Spirit and the people. They themselves present with trust issues, which leads to becoming socially distant speaking to the people from their flesh wounds. Remember, hurt people hurt others, but we can't operate as the leaders in offenses and bringing offenses.

The Bible reminds us in Luke 17:1b, "Offences would come, but woe through whom they come through." Matthew 18:6 reads, "But if you cause one of these little ones who trusts in me to fall into sin, it would be better for you to have a large millstone tied around your neck and be drowned in the depths of the sea." This scripture warns you of the pending consequences. Therefore, leaders or whatever capacity you are leading from must watch what you say and think about how you treat the people, mainly those of the household of faith.

In this twenty-first century church, there is so much competition occurring, which causes a negative view of the real church of God in Christ. You see leaders trying to outdo the next leader, presenting their ministry almost in a business sense. In other words, being a leader has become lucrative, as they operate a financial institution and multimillion-dollar business. We now have various ways you can give unto the work, but people become quite offensive when there is a full ATM machine in the church. Now don't get me wrong. I know we are trying to modernize to keep up with technology, but in this, we have made the people more comfortable and less responsible and accountable.

Now let me give this transparent moment. Many times, I haven't had any cash on me, but I didn't go anywhere without my plastic. So, this method also helped me to do what is right in a different way. Technology affords us the ability to do things differently; however, we must be also mindful not to allow technology and the flexibility of this change to become a distraction to the souls of men.

We used to have prayer lines that drew people to repentance, turning them back to the love of God. Now we have prophetic lines that prostitute the people for their wages. The church was given free gifts to bless the body of Christ, not to be used to harm them or for personal gain.

Now listen, I truly believe that giving lends to my living. Luke 6:28a says, "Give and it shall come back to you press down, shaken together and running over shall men give unto your bosom." Genesis 8:22a says, "While the earth remaineth there will be seedtime and harvest." Galatians 6:7 reads, "Be not deceived; God is not mocked, whatsoever a man soweth, that shall he also reap." Proverbs 10:22 says, "The blessing of the Lord makes rich, and he adds no sorrow to it."

We see scripture that we should give of our means to bless the work of the Lord. However, the problem thus even becomes almost strenuous and cruel in the eyes of the believer because of the motives and intentions of the receiver, which has in many cases become numb to the best interests and sacrifices of the giver. Yes, I get it and understand 1 Timothy 5:18, "Muzzle not the ox that treads out the corn." But when the yoke is placed on your neck as a burden because your sacrifice may be pleasing and acceptable unto God but isn't good enough for the receiver, then it becomes problematic.

There was an instant when Jesus was overlooking the offering in Luke 21. Jesus observed all the wealthy, well-to-do people bringing their big offerings. This woman was known as a poor widow. She brought all she had, which was two mites. Jesus didn't say a word concerning those who had it or much to give, but it is then interesting to note that He made mention of this poor widow. He said in verse 3, "This poor widow has put in more than all." What a place to put a praise. Listen, you don't have to keep up with the Jones, Smiths, or Williams. Just give as 2 Corinthians 9: 6 – 7 says "But this I say, He which soweth sparingly shall reap also sparingly: and he which soweth bountifully shall reap also bountifully. Every man according as he purposeth in his heart, so let him give; not grudgingly, or of necessity: for God loveth a cheerful giver."

Reminiscing, there was a time when the visiting preacher would travel to preach, even when there were only a few members in attendance. They had a vision of souls being added to the kingdom, deliverance and healing taking place, and God being totally glorified. Now, some preachers have extended riders that consist of premium coverage to include, but certainly not limited to, their airfare, car rental/gas, five-star hotel accommodations for them and their crew, and food allotment attached. I've worked behind the scenes administratively, handling some of these requests personally where the preacher requested to know how many people they could expect in attendance and how many churches was coming together for the event.

They needed to have specific equipment such as a Hammond at 8800 keys, a lapel mic, and a specific brand of water. A requested honorarium in addition to at least half of the main offering that was received would become theirs. They hyped up the people, but the people left broke and broken. One word: Wow! It seems that we have come a long way in remembering the church of yesteryears, but some of those practices are still visible today even in the real church of God in Christ.

Church was a place where the pastor's sole vision lined up with the Great Commission. The pastor always ministered to the rejected, downtrodden, wounded, oppressed, and possessed. Church was a place where people used to come for salvation, deliverance, healing, and encouragement. People didn't wait until a calamity occurred, death happened, their child got locked up, and the sorts. Church then was very much family-oriented as we united as the family of God in Christ.

Unfortunately, some of the twenty-first century preachers and congregants have the wrong focus and purpose for why they even come to church today. There was a time when we got saved and came to church to serve, love our fellowman and learn the ways of God. However, many have ulteria motives of why they are at church now. We used to have the testimony "I was glad when they said unto me let us go into the house of the Lord, but sadly, some people just don't feel that way anymore. It is almost out of habit and formalities nowadays because of the private agenda for personal gain and status.

Church used to be the place where they said everybody is somebody now. The script has changed to everybody wants to be somebody. Psalm 145:4 says, "One generation will praise thy works to another and shall declare his mighty acts." The problem is not with the scriptures; it is with the people who say they were called to proclaim, declare, and decree the word, but seem to only do so when being observed, prodded, and coached.

If the previous generation did not follow the complete

instruction given by the Lord, how shall a people (a nation) be saved for real? Are we just going through the motions and forgetting our assignment? Where is the real church of God in Christ?

When a generation fails to pass the baton of good works in righteousness and holiness to the next generation, we end up raising a generation of hirelings who don't know what it means to walk by faith and not by sight. Unfortunately, people have been taught about the organization, denominational founders, and the protocol of the church, but not the character and integrity of the church. So many know flow of church, but lack intimacy with the God of the church.

We have lacked in many ways of living by precept and example of the scriptures. However, we can no longer say one thing and do another. Souls are weighing in the balance. "Multitudes, multitudes in the valley of decision" (Joel 3:14). Romans 8:19 tells us, "The creation is eagerly awaiting the revelation of God's children." In other words, the world, the hurting, the hopeless, the helpless, those in bondage, and those in sickness and experiencing sorrows of every kind is waiting on the manifestation of the real church of God in Christ to rise up. Now is the time!

It may seem that the same thing is being said, but repetition is a good teacher, so even now I speak prophetically to you. Yes, you! I declare and decree for the real church of God in Christ to rise up. Assume your position and manifest as the *Ekklesia*, the call-out assembly according to the scriptures. It's time that we get back to our priorities and our Lord's purpose. It is vitally important that we who call ourselves the church of the living God get back to our roots and function of why we have our being.

Can I tell you we don't look back to go back? We look back to learn so we can know how to proceed. In retrospect, the church of old revealed several vital and riveting truths to us. We learn of many who have went before us in power and demonstration of the spoken word. There were many televangelists who ministered to the masses by way of the airways. They had one message (though expressed in different ways) that drew people to the love of Jesus, which obliged them to decide to accept this sacrificial gift of love. One of the most prestigious televangelists was Billy Graham. Billy Graham's ministry started in his younger years, compelling people to decide to accept the gift of salvation through faith in Jesus Christ.

By the year of 1993, he had preached to more than 2.5 million people. Now when you tune in to the twenty-first century televangelists, many of the messages have strayed away from the central purpose and theme that the real church of God in Christ should be reverberating. You hear more about gimmicks and sending money on the many streams out there than hearing of the gospel of Jesus Christ.

Now don't get me wrong. I believe in the prosperity of the saints according to the word, but not at the expense of the people for gluttonous increase. The word "prosperity" according to Merriam-Webster means "to become strong and flourishing."

I believe with the concurrence of scripture in Psalm 35:27, "Let them shout for joy, and be glad, that favour my righteous cause: yea, let them say continually, Let the LORD be magnified, which hath pleasure in the prosperity of his servant." For the scripture saith in 1 Timothy 5:18 "Thou shalt not muzzle the ox that treadeth out the corn. And, the labourer is worthy of his reward. Paul said according to Romans 15:27, "For if the Gentiles have been made partakers of their spiritual things, their duty is also to minister unto them in carnal things."

Paul follows up this statement in 1 Corinthians 9:11 (emergency) if I could paraphrase, "If men and women of God sow into us spiritual things (which cause us to grow and develop both spiritually and naturally), we should certainly sow into them monetarily." It's time that the true church of God in Christ increases in this area, bridging the gap economically for kingdom business where nothing is broken, missing, or lacking. There are churches springing up everywhere, which seems to be trending to the forefront of what in some minds is now considered real ministry, on the cutting edge. You can hardly walk one block or drive one mile without seeing at least two to four churches.

Now some of these churches are called ministries. However, the concern is that you have a handful of people, and they, for the most part, are the family members of the leader. It's been months, if not years, that those same few family members are still the only ones sitting on the pews. However, some have gotten it twisted, thinking that the power of God won't fall in such a place, but I beg to differ. You see, I've been in the small, medium, and even mega ministries that some don't possess the purpose or power of the real church of God in Christ has.

Regrettably, some feel that if your church doesn't have thousands of people seated in the pews, then it is almost looked down upon by religious mindsets of today. I had a conversation with some of the elders of today as we shared in what the real church of God in Christ possesses. Zechariah 4:10 tells us, "Not to despise the days of small beginnings." Job 8:7 encourages us to know that "though your beginning be small your latter will flourish and increase." Regardless of what the real church of God in Christ has or will experience, go through, or must fight through, they will always emerge victoriously!

Now the observation of the church of old was that of humility. I believe when you know where you came from, the struggles you've faced and endured with the help of the Lord right there in your community storefront church, it often keeps you humbled.

There was a time when people joined the local neighborhood church where they were faithfully committed to the cause. Sunday school, Bible study, and all the other things offered in that local church excited the people to constantly and consistently self-evaluate to see if their lives were in satisfactory condition to the purpose and sharing of the love of God with others. They knew that the call to ministry was greater than their personal worldviews.

It was important then and even more so now to be fertile in producing fruit, as found in Galatians 5:22–23 "But the fruit of the Spirit is love, joy, peace, longsuffering, gentleness, goodness, faith, meekness, temperance: against such there is no law." Prepared and ready fruitfulness produces regeneration. Regeneration, in its simplest form, means change. I knew my life had changed in many ways by my spending time in the word and prayer. I remember one experience from prayer. The Holy Spirit told me that the only way I could commit to the earthly leader here was because I was first submitted to God. In other words, in order to commit yourself to a man or woman of God, you must first be submitted to the lover of your soul. The benefit is that He will cause you to be a new creature, producing fruits of repentance unto righteousness.

Now during this process, I had to go through a purification and pruning process. To prune, for the lack of a better word, means to be cut. I had to allow the Spirit of God to cut me and stay under long enough for Him to then heal me. The word itself is a double-edged sword. It will perform surgery, going in and stitching up your wounds coming out. However, oftentimes a scar is left as a reminder so we can maintain the gift of remembrance. Jesus allows us to see what we are really made of when He put us to a test while developing our spiritual character.

Jesus knows what He has invested in us, but warns us to "beware of false prophets, which come to you in sheep's clothing, but inwardly they are ravening wolves. Ye shall know them by their fruits. Do men gather grapes of thorns, or figs of thistles? Even so every, good tree bringeth forth good fruit; but a corrupt tree bringeth forth evil fruit. A good tree cannot bring forth evil fruit, neither can a corrupt tree bring forth good fruit. Every tree that bringeth not forth good fruit is hewn down and cast into the fire. Wherefore by their fruits ye shall know them" (Matthew 7:15–20).

The tragedy of our modern day is that so many have claimed to be born again yet without producing the corresponding fruits. 2 Corinthians 5:17 says "Therefore if any man be in Christ, he is a new creature: old things are passed away; behold all things are become new." So in this, we understand that the radical inward change wrought in rebirth produces fruits that should display an equivalent outward change in the behavior of the person who is born again.

In John 3, Nicodemus came to Jesus by night. He was a man of authority, yet secretly he hungered for more of God. This lets us know that no matter a person's status, from the highest office to the man or woman living under a bridge, when you hunger for more, you will seek out the one who can fill you to overflow.

CHAPTER 17

Saved by Grace through Faith

Listen, we don't have faith in faith, but faith in God and His word. You see, the word is big enough to reach you right where you are. It's so wide that you can't go around it, so long you can't go before it, so low you can't go under it, and so high you can go over it. However, through the word, you can go to deeper heights, breaths, lengths, and widths. The word comes in seed form cultivated in the hearts of those who receive it by faith.

The apostle inserts Ephesians 2:8–10, "By grace are we saved by faith and not that of ourselves, it is the gift of God not of works, lest any man should boast for we are his workmanship, created in Christ Jesus unto good works, which God hath before ordained that we should walk in them." What life-changing power we possess when we understand we can do no thing without God. We find that Jesus will meet you at the point of your need and pull you out the muck and mire as we allow His grace to uphold us and His right hand to keep us from falling, but you must upgrade from the flesh to the Spirit, according to Galatians 5.

"The carnal (natural or fleshly) man or can't receive, perceive or understand the things of the Spirit for they are foolishness (folly) unto him and he cannot know them because they are spiritually discerned" (1 Corinthians 2:14). Jesus's grace extended to Nicodemus. Jesus began to give him that which is spiritual, stating "Except a man be born again, he cannot see the kingdom of God," yet he comprehended it not.

Many have acquired knowledge that is mere legalistic and law-bound, leaving the people to always be reminded of sinfulness and bondage. However, we are reminded in 1 Corinthians 8:1, "knowledge puffeth up, but charity (LOVE) edified." Nevertheless, legalism or holding fast to the law won't work because we no longer live under the law but under grace. Titus 2:11a says, "The grace of God has appeared that offers salvation to all people." Ephesians 4:7 reads, "But to each one of us grace has been given as Christ apportioned it."

So though Nicodemus' comprehension was that of a fleshly mind, his hunger for something greater than the law, education, title, and position caused him to continue the dialog as he responded to Jesus's question with two other questions, "How can a man be born again when he is old? Can he come through his mother's womb again?"

Know this: when you encounter the presence of the Lord, your appetite will change, and Jesus will cause you to thirst and hunger. Matthew 5:6 encourages us to know that "they that thirst and hunger after righteousness shall be filled."

This is a promise to you and your children, even to those who are afar. Why? God so loves us that He gave us the best He had as an offering for our salvation (John 3:16). Jesus took the conversation to another level in John 3:5 – 7 by saying, "Verily, verily, I say unto thee, Except a man be born of water and of the Spirit, he cannot enter into the kingdom. He expounded saying that which is born of the flesh is flesh; and that which is born of the Spirit is spirit. Marvel not that I said unto thee, Ye must be born again." This is a "must know." Many have gone down in the water but have not the Spirit of Christ. I've heard someone say, "Gone down a dry devil and came up a wet devil." Know this! Water baptism doesn't bring salvation. We get baptized not to get saved, but because we are saved. However, this helps us to be identified with Christ's death, burial, and resurrection.

Someone may want to know, "How do you know you have the Spirit of Christ?" That's a good question. The response is simple. Having the Spirit of Christ produces righteous fruit as found in Galatians 5:22–23. It also produces the attributes of Christ in the heart and minds of His servants. The Spirit causes you to see things God's way and not your way or others. Proverbs 14:12 says, "There is a way that seemeth right to man, but the end thereof leads to destruction/death." Proverbs 19:21 reads, "There are many plans/devices in a man's heart/mind, but the counsel of the Lord will stand."

Nonetheless, Romans 8:19 states, "For the earnest expectation of the creature waiteth for the manifestation of the sons of God." We're back to where it all started: line upon line, precept upon precept, and here and there a little. It's from Genesis to Revelation and from the origin to the originator and authenticator. It's what we are and what we are not. Our responsibility, mission, order, and the symbols thereof still reveal that we are still here.

The visibility of its glorious power fully identified through the emergence of the real church of God in Christ is still rising. As I wrap up this portion of the book, I want to leave you with this final scripture found in 2 Thessalonians 2:15–17,

"Therefore, brethren, stand fast, and hold the traditions which ye have been taught, whether by word, or our epistle. Now our Lord Jesus Christ himself, and God, even our Father, which hath loved us, and hath given [us] everlasting consolation and good hope through grace, comfort your hearts, and stablish you in every good word and work."

Here's why. Psalm 50:2 says, "For out of ZION, the perfection of beauty, God will shine forth." It's time to show up and be accounted for. There is much more to be said about the real church of God in Christ. Where is it? I'll tell you where it is. It's in you!

Will the real church of God in Christ stand up?

REFERENCES

"Bible.Is." bible.is.

"BibleCite.com." www.biblecite.com.

"BibleGateway." www.biblegateway.com.

"Bibles.net." www.bibles.net.

"BibleStudies.org." www.redletterbible.com.

"Billy Graham," en.wikipedia.org/wiki/Billy Graham.

"Blue Letter Bible." www.blueletterbible.org.

"Crosswalk.com." www.crosswalk.com.

"Encyclopedia Britannica." www.EncyclopediaBritannica.org.

"Jesus Film Project." www.jesusfilm.org.

"Joshua Project." www.joshuaproject.com.

"Living Web." www.livingweb.com.

"T.D. Jakes, "Your gift will carry you where your character can't keep you! "A Twitter post" November 22, 2015, Twitter. com/T.D. Jakes

"Merriam-Webster." www.Merriam-Webster.com. "YouVersion." www.youversion.com.

Strong's Exhaustive Concordance of the Bible, James Strong LLD, STD, Copyright 1995, Thomas Nelson Publishers.

The American Heritage Dictionary, 2nd College ed., 1982.

The King James Bible, Oxford Standard Text, 1769.

The New American Standard Bible-Redletter, Moody Press, 1978. www.gospelcom.net www.biblegateway.com

Printed in the United States
By Bookmasters